The Truth Abou

The Chicago Trib

Frederick Starr

Alpha Editions

This edition published in 2024

ISBN : 9789362510150

Design and Setting By
Alpha Editions
www.alphaedis.com
Email - info@alphaedis.com

As per information held with us this book is in Public Domain.
This book is a reproduction of an important historical work. Alpha Editions uses the best technology to reproduce historical work in the same manner it was first published to preserve its original nature. Any marks or number seen are left intentionally to preserve its true form.

Contents

PREFACE .... - 1 -
I. .... - 3 -
II. .... - 12 -
III. .... - 19 -
IV. .... - 24 -
V. .... - 28 -
VI. .... - 33 -
VII. .... - 38 -
VIII. .... - 43 -
IX. .... - 52 -
X. .... - 56 -
XI. .... - 60 -
XII. .... - 66 -
XIII. .... - 71 -
XIV. .... - 75 -
XV. .... - 81 -

PREFACE

WHEN I returned to America, I had decided to express no opinion upon the public and political questions of the Congo Free State. Having found conditions there quite different from what I had expected, it was impossible for me to state my actual impressions without danger of antagonizing or offending some whom I valued as friends. Hence, on landing at New York, I refused to say anything upon those matters to several reporters who interviewed me. A little later, the *Chicago Tribune* asked me to write upon these subjects, urging the importance of the whole matter to our nation, and leaving me entire freedom in viewpoint and mode of treatment. In response to its request, I prepared a series of articles, which appeared in successive issues from January 20 to February 3, 1907.

The articles were received with general interest, and many asked that they should be reprinted in book form. I felt that they were of momentary interest only, and as I have much other Congo matter for books and pamphlets—more directly in the line of my professional work—I was inclined not to reprint them. But I soon found myself the subject of bitter attack. Malicious and untrue statements were made regarding me and my motives. I have concluded, therefore, that it is best that my articles should be accessible to all who are interested. What I wrote, I am ready to defend. I am not ready to be judged from misquotations, or condemned for what I never wrote. Hence this book.

I am not personally responsible for the title—*The Truth about the Congo*. Although I believe all my statements are true, I should not have selected that title for my articles. No man can say all that is true on any subject, and I do not arrogate to myself a monopoly in truth-telling, either about the Congo or any other topic. But after my announcement under that heading, I decided to let it stand. I preferred some less assertive title, but I am content. So I use the same title for this book. The headlines of the articles, however, I have suppressed. They were not of my preparation and did not adequately suggest the matter or the treatment. The articles are reprinted with no changes except corrections in spelling, punctuation, or mistaken words.

No man more desires the happiness and progress of the Congo natives than do I. I know them pretty well. I am their friend; they are my friends. I shall be glad if what I here present makes them and their cause better known to thoughtful and sympathetic men and women, Mere emotion, however violent, will not help them. Stubborn refusal to recognize and encourage reforms, which have been seriously undertaken for their betterment, will only harm them.

I.

January 20, 1907.

MY own interest in the Congo Free State began at the St. Louis exposition. As is well known, that exposition made a special feature of groups of representatives of tribes from various parts of the world. These natives dressed in native dress, lived in native houses, and so far as possible reproduced an accurate picture of the daily life to which they were accustomed in their homes.

Among the groups there brought together was one of Congo natives. This group was commonly known as the pygmy group, though but four out of the nine members composing it made claims to be such. The group was brought by Mr. S. P. Verner, at one time missionary to the Congo, who was engaged by the exposition to make a special journey into central Africa to procure it. Four members of the group were Batua, the others were large blacks representing the Bakuba and Baluba.

The idea of visiting Africa was one which I had never seriously entertained, but in the study of these Congolese it seemed to me that there were interesting questions the solution of which would well repay a visit. The consequence was, that I determined to visit the Congo Free State—and specifically that part of the state from which these natives had been brought.

About this time I received considerable literature from the Congo Reform Association at Boston, the reading of which had its influence in deciding me to undertake the expedition.

After reading this literature I started for the Congo, fully prepared to see all kinds of horrors. I supposed that mutilations, cruelties, and atrocities of the most frightful kinds would everywhere present themselves. I expected to find a people everywhere suffering, mourning, and in unhappiness.

My errand, however, was not that of a searcher after all these dreadful things, but purely that of a student of human races, with definite questions for investigation.

I may say that my opportunities for forming an opinion of conditions in the Congo have been exceptional. Mine was no hasty journey, but a tarry in the country extending over more than one year.

While my original plan was to spend the greater portion of my time in the district ruled by the Bakuba chief, Ndombe, with but a short period in other parts of the state, I had decided before reaching the mouth of the Congo to more evenly distribute my time, and to see far more of the Congo proper than I at first intended. As a consequence, I went first into the Kasai district, where I spent four months, after which, returning to Leopoldville, I went up the main river to the head of navigation, and even beyond, to Ponthierville, the terminus of the newly built line of railroad. We also went up the Aruwimi, to the famous Yambuya camp, where the navigation of that river is interrupted by cataracts.

I have, therefore, seen not only the lower Congo, which has been so frequently visited in recent years, but traveled thousands of miles upon the great river and two of its most important tributaries.

In this extended journey I came into constant contact with representatives of the three groups of white men who live in the Congo Free State—state officials, missionaries, and traders. I had repeated conversations with them all, and have heard opinions upon the Congo State from these diverse points of view.

My position with reference to Congo matters is peculiar, doubly so. I may even say it is unique. My journey was made at my own expense; I was not the representative of any institution, society, or body. I was without instructions, and my observations were untrammeled by any demands or conditions from outside.

While I am under many and weighty obligations to scores of state officials, missionaries, and traders, I am not prevented from speaking my mind in regard to any and every matter. Both to the missionaries, state officials, and traders I paid board and lodging at every stopping point—with the single exception of one American mission station—a fact which leaves me freedom. While the state facilitated my visit and my work in many ways, I was not, at any time, in relations with it of such a kind as to interfere with free observations or free expression. I made this entirely clear on my first visit to the state authorities at Brussels, and it was understood by them that I should speak freely and frankly of everything which I should see. On their part, the state authorities expressed the liveliest satisfaction that an independent American traveler should visit the Congo Free State, and said that they did not wish anything concealed or attenuated, as they felt sure that such a visit as mine could only do them good.

I have said that my position was doubly peculiar. I was not only independent and untrammeled in observation and expression, but my personal attitude to the whole question of colonization and administration by a foreign power, of natives, is radical. Personally I dislike the effort to elevate, civilize, remake a people. I should prefer to leave the African as he was before white contact. It is my belief that there is no people so weak or so degraded as to be incapable of self-government. I believe that every people is happier and better with self-government, no matter how unlike our own form that government may be. I feel that no nation is good enough, or wise enough, or sufficiently advanced to undertake the elevation and civilization of a "lower" people. Still less do I approve the exploitation of a native population by outsiders for their own benefit. Nor do I feel that even the development of British trade warrants interference with native life, customs, laws, and lands. I know, however, that these views are unpopular and heretical.

In the series of articles, then, which I have been asked to prepare, I shall try to take the standpoint of the practical man, the business man, the man of affairs, the philanthropist, the missionary. All these agree that civilized folk have a perfect right to interfere with any native tribe too weak to resist their encroachment. They agree that it is perfectly right to trample under foot native customs, institutions, ideas—to change and modify, to introduce innovations, either to develop trade, to exploit a country, to elevate a race, or to save souls. I am forced, then, to look at Congo matters from the point of view of these eminently practical men.

Of course, I saw much to criticise. It is true that there are floggings, and chain-gangs, and prisons. I have seen them all repeatedly. But there are floggings, chain-gangs, and prisons in the United States. Mutilations are so rare that one must seek for them; and I had too much else to do. There is taxation—yes, heavy taxation—a matter which I shall discuss quite fully further on. And in connection with taxation there is forced labor, a matter which, of course, I disapprove, but it appears as just to all the groups of eminently practical men to whom I have referred. There are, no doubt, hostages in numbers, but I saw less than a dozen. And the whole matter of hostages is one which merits careful and candid discussion. And I know that in many a large district the population is much smaller than in former times. The causes of this diminution in numbers are many and various, and to them I shall return.

Flogging, chain-gang, prison, mutilation, heavy taxation, hostages, depopulation—all these I saw, but at no time and at no place were they so flagrant as to force themselves upon attention. And of frightful outrages, such as I had expected to meet everywhere, I may almost say there was nothing. It is, of course, but fair to state that I was not in the district of the A. B. I. R. I cannot believe, however, that conditions in that district are so appalling as the newspaper reports would indicate.

On the contrary, I found at many places a condition of the negro population far happier than I had dreamed it possible. The negro of the Congo—or Bantu, if you please—is a born trader. He is imitative to a degree. He is acquisitive, and charmed with novelties. He is bright and quick, remarkably intelligent. He readily acquires new languages, and it is no uncommon thing to find a Congo Bantu who can speak six or seven languages besides his own. In disposition variable and emotional, he quickly forgets his sorrow. I saw hundreds of natives who were working happily, living in good houses, dressing in good clothes of European stuff and pattern, and saving property. That this number will rapidly increase I have no doubt.

And now, on my return, after having many of my preconceived ideas completely shattered, and feeling on the whole that things in Congoland are not so bad, and that improvement is the order of the day, I am startled to find the greatest excitement. Pages of newspapers are filled with stories of atrocities, many of which never happened, some of which are ancient, and a part of which, recent in date, are true.

I find a fierce excitement about the Belgium lobby, vigorous resolutions presented in the senate, and the President of the United States outrunning his most urgent supporters and advisers, ready to take some drastic action to ameliorate the conditions of the suffering millions in the Congo Free State. The surprise is so much the greater, as my latest information regarding the American official attitude had been gained from the letter written by Secretary Root some months ago.

What can be the reason of such prodigious and sudden change?

What has happened in the Congo since April to produce the present state of mind? What is the motive underlying the bitter attacks upon Leopold and the Free State which he established? Is it truly humanitarian? Or are the laudable impulses and praiseworthy sympathies of two great people being used for hidden and sinister ends of politics?

I do not claim infallibility. I do claim that my having spent a year in the Congo Free State, independently, should qualify me to express opinions on the conditions. I have heard both sides. I have traveled thousands of miles in Congo territory. I have visited natives of twenty-eight different tribes. No interference has been placed in my way. I have gone where I pleased, and when and how I pleased. No preparations have been made with reference to my visits. I believe no changes in practice have been produced by my presence.

In the series of articles before us it is my intention to present in detail what I have seen, and much of what I have heard, in the Congo Independent State. I may make errors, but I shall tell no intentional falsehoods. I shall criticise what deserves criticism. I shall praise what is praiseworthy. I trust that those who are interested in forming a true idea of Congo conditions may find something useful in my observations.

At this point it is necessary for us to know something of the Congo native himself. In Dark Africa—for northern Africa is and always has been a white man's country—there are three negro or negroid masses. There is little doubt that the original inhabitants of the continent were dwarf people, ancestors of the pygmies of the high Ituri forest, and the Batua of the upper Kasai.

To-day the pygmies are mere fragments, scattered and separated, but retaining with tenacity their ancient life. They are the same to-day as they were 5,000 years ago, when they were objects of interest to the old Egyptians. Little in stature, scrawny in form, with a face shrewd, cunning, and sly, the pygmy is a hunter. With his bows and poisoned arrows he kills the game of the forests and makes no pretense of doing aught in agriculture. He is universally feared by the large blacks in the neighborhood of whose towns he settles. He trades his game for agricultural products with his large neighbors.

In the Soudan and neighboring parts of western Africa live the true negroes, notable for their thick lips, projecting lower faces, and dark skin.

Throughout southern Africa we find a group of populations much lighter in color, and on the whole more attractive in appearance, than the true negro. These tribes, plainly related in language, are no doubt of one blood, and are called Bantu. The name is unfortunate, as the word bantu simply means "men" in that group of languages. Practically the whole of the Congo population are Bantu—there being almost no true negroes and but few pygmies in the area.

It would seem as if the Congo native should be so well known by this time that the current description of him in the text-books would be accurate; yet, at least in two respects, these stereotyped accounts are wrong. The Congo Bantu are not long-headed, and it is not true that they differ from the real negro in the absence of a characteristic and disagreeable odor. There are scores of Bantu tribes, each with its own language and minor peculiarities in appearance and life. It would be untrue to say that all smell badly, but I have often wished the writers of the books could be shut up a while in the same room with, for example, a group of Bobangi. It is certain that no type of African smells worse.

It would be, however, a mistake to think that the Bantu are dirty. Far from it. I have repeatedly observed my carriers, when we came to some brook in the forest, set their loads aside, strip themselves when necessary, and bathe in the fresh cool water. They are scrupulous in attention to their teeth, and use, often several times a day, a little stick of wood, somewhat larger than a lead-pencil, shredded at one end, to clean their teeth. The instrument, by the way, serves its purpose far better than our own toothbrushes.

According to his tribe, the Bantu may be short, medium, or tall. King Ndombe of the Bakuba measures six feet three in stature, and is well-built, though not heavy. Among the Bakuba, Baluba, Batetela, and Bakete, tall statures are common. It is rare, however, that the Bantu present what we would call finely developed forms; their chest is often flat and sunken; their shoulders not well thrown backward; and the musculature of their back, their chest, arms, and legs, is poor. Of course, there are exceptions, and one sometimes sees magnificently developed specimens. In the lower Congo, where on the whole the men are shorter, they make excellent carriers. In the old caravan days the standard burden was sixty or seventy pounds, and a man would carry it without difficulty all the working day. The Kasai tribes are poor carriers and indifferent workers. The chopbox of sixty pounds weight, which the lower Congo man shoulders easily and carries without complaint, will be slung to a pole to be borne by two carriers among the Baluba.

In life the Bantu populations, so far as the Congo is concerned, present notable general uniformity. The general pattern is the same everywhere, though there are local and tribal differences of minor sort. Thus, almost every tribe has its own tribal marks cut into the flesh of face or body.

Similarly, the members of one tribe may be distinguished by their mode of dressing the hair. To a less degree, the form to which the teeth are chipped and broken mark tribal differences. It may almost be said that no two tribes in all the Congo build houses that are just alike, and almost every tribe has its characteristic mode of arranging the houses in a group. Thus, in one tribe the houses will be arranged in continuous lines, one on each side of a straight road; in another the houses may be grouped around the three sides of a square, the group belonging to a single chieftain and being succeeded in the village by other similar groups of buildings; in another the houses will be arranged in two curved lines, leaving the open space in the center of the village oval or elliptical. The chairs or stools of one tribe will differ in form and decoration from those of another; so will the wooden spoons, the stirring-sticks, the combs, the dress and ornaments.

The Congo natives for the most part still lead a tribal life. A chief is the head of a little community clustered about him. He may not be the chief of a whole village; for example, at Bomanih, on the Aruwimi, there are three chiefs. Each one has his own cluster of houses, and though the three clusters are arranged continuously in two, parallel, straight lines, every native of the village knows precisely where the domain of the individual chief ends or begins.

The power and authority of the chief has been greatly weakened by contact with the whites, but he still retains great influence. At least over the members of his own household, including, of course, his slaves, he had the power of life and death. In large affairs, interesting a considerable number of people, he usually acted on the advice and opinion of his fellows as expressed in a village or tribal palaver. The chief was, and still is, distinguished from the common people by his dress and ornaments. He is usually a man of wealth, and has a considerable number of people actually dependent upon him, subject to his orders, and a force upon which he can depend in case of war or trouble.

When I first entered the Congo my heart sank, for it seemed as if the native life was gone. In fact, in letters written from Matadi I doubted whether I had not come too late for aught of interest. My spirits began to revive, however, with the railroad journey from Matadi to Leopoldville. Groups of natives, with scanty dress and barbaric ornaments, replaced those who at Matadi and its neighborhood gathered at the station to see the train pass.

In my first walk from the mission house where I lodged at Leo, within three minutes' walk of the mission I found a little cluster of Bateke houses which, with its inhabitants, much delighted me.

Almost naked women, with abundance of beads and teeth hung at their necks as ornaments, with hair elaborately dressed and bodies smeared with red camwood powder, squatted on the ground, were making native pottery in graceful forms.

In the shade in front of the door of one of the houses was a true barbarian, lord of the place. By rare good luck he spoke a little English, so that we were able to carry on a conversation. When I asked him who the women were, he replied that they were his wives. I think there were three of them, and it was my first introduction to African polygamy. Each of these women occupied a separate house. Each of them had a garden patch in which she worked. All of them contributed to the importance and support of their husband.

Polygamy, of course, prevails throughout Dark Africa. But do not misunderstand me. I do not use the word "dark" to characterize polygamy. It is a settled institution which seems to work quite well. Later on I saw the wives of Ndombe, thirty-four in number. Ndombe is a really important chief, but compared with some whom we met or of whom we heard in the Upper Congo, he was but scantily equipped. Sixty, seventy, a hundred, or hundreds of wives and female slaves, which count for much the same, are in possession of great chieftains. There is, of course, always one favorite or principal wife. When Ndombe used to come, as he frequently did, to my house to see the stereoscopic pictures, he frequently brought his favorite wife with him. She was a pretty creature—young and plump, graceful and modest. She wore good cloth and any quantity of beads and brass arm and leg rings.

In every case the women of a chief or rich man live in separate houses, each having her own. Until a man is married he is but little thought of. The greater the number of his wives, the more important he becomes. As each one cultivates a field and does other productive labor, it will be seen that the man with the most wives is the richest man.

The man has his own house, but visits and lives in the houses of his wives in turn. The child in Africa is rarely weaned before it is two or three years old, and during the period of time when a child is unweaned the father has no marital relations with the woman. On the whole, there is less quarreling among the wives of a polygamic husband than one would expect. Bantu women, however, are often termagants, as women elsewhere, and at times the chief's house group is lively.

Domestic slavery still flourishes. The state, of course, has done much to end the actual slave trade for supplying white men and Arabs. It is, however, difficult to deal with the matter of domestic slavery, and in fact is scarcely worth the candle.

Every chief or man of any consequence has slaves. Calamba, my interpreter, at Ndombe, though a young fellow, probably not more than 25, had two. It is rare that the lot of the domestic slave is unhappy. It is usually women or children who are bought, and they are treated in all respects as if members of the family. Little is required of them in the way of work and service, and they must absolutely be provided for by the master, who is also frequently responsible before the public for their misdeeds. Formerly, of course, there was the possibility of being killed upon a festal occasion, the accession of the chief to increased power, or to grace his funeral. Within those districts where the state has a firm hold and strong influence this possibility is done away with, and the most serious disadvantage in being a slave is thus removed. Slaves may become rich men, and not infrequently themselves hold slaves.

Perhaps the most striking characteristic of the Bantu, as of the true negro, is his emotionality—one instant joyous, the next in tears. Vowing vengeance for an injury to-day, he is on the happiest terms with his injurer to-morrow. He laughs, sings, dances. Of all the introductions of the white man, perhaps the accordion is the favorite. Men use it, but women play it constantly. Most of them play one song piece only, and one may hear it from one end of the state to the other at every hour of the day and night. Of course, there are native instruments in plenty, drums of every size and form, from the small hand drum, made by stretching a skin across an earthen pot three or four inches in diameter, up to the great cylindrical, horizontal drum made by hollowing logs a yard in diameter and ten feet long. There are horns, fifes, pipes, and whistles, and a great series of stringed instruments, ranging from the musical bow with but one cord to lutes with ten or twelve. Of course, the instrumental music goes with the dancing.

The native is born to dance. Babies, two or three years old, dance with their elders. Men dance together; women have their special forms; but in the majority of cases the two sexes dance together. There is, however, nothing like our waltzes or round dancing, individuals keeping themselves separate.

The dances are most frequent and lively when the moon is growing. On moonlight nights hundreds of people—men, women, and children—gather at dusk, and to the noise of drums dance wildly, often till morning. It is no uncommon thing for people working on plantations to work all day and dance almost all night, and this day after day. While some of the dances are extremely graceful, most of them are obscene and are followed often by frightful orgies.

One thing greatly interested me. Had I been asked before my trip to Africa about the cake-walk—a form of amusement which I love to see—I should have said that it originated in America among the black folk of our southern states. But no, the cake-walk is no American invention. In every part of the Congo one may see it—even in regions where white influence has seldom penetrated. The American cake-walk is an immigrant.

The Bantu child is wonderfully precocious. This precocity displays itself in everything. The children run about with perfect freedom, instead of tottering along, one unsteady step after another, as our children of the same age. They speak astonishingly soon. A babe in arms eats solid food—notwithstanding the fact that it is not weaned until two or three years of age—shockingly early. The little child imitates the every action of its older friends. Children of four or five, in shrewdness, comprehension, and intelligence, are like our ten-year-olds. This precocity suggests the fact of early ripening. As a fact, boys of sixteen and girls of thirteen are frequently ready for marriage. A man of twenty-five is in the prime of life, a man of thirty aged, and on the whole the term of life closes at thirty-five.

II.

January 21, 1907.

LIFE is easy in the tropics. Wants are few. A house to live in can be built in a few hours. Food can be gathered or produced with little labor. Dress is needless. Where life is easy there is little impulse to labor.

The chief incentive to the Bantu to work is to secure the wherewithal to buy a wife. The boy, who, through a careless, happy childhood, has done naught but play, begins to think of settling down. But to have a wife he must have money or its equivalent. So he goes to work. It may require a year or more before he has the pieces of cloth which are necessary for the purchase of his desired loved one. The same stimulus which impelled him to labor for one wife may prod him to efforts for others. But with the establishment of a home, and the purchase of two or three wives to care for him and produce him wealth, his work is done. From fourteen years to twenty-five is his working period. Before that time a child, after that time he is a man of means. What wealth comes later comes through the women and their labor, and through trade.

We have already stated that the Bantu is notably acquisitive. Wealth, apart from women and slaves, is counted mostly in cloth. One of the chief aims in life is to accumulate cloth, not for use as clothing, but as evidence of wealth and for the final display when the man dies and is buried. Among the Lower Congo tribes the dead body is wrapped in piece after piece of cloth, until the body disappears in a mass of wrappings made of scores of pieces, each piece consisting of eight or sixteen yards, as the case may be. Young men have cloth, and it is most interesting to look through the boxes of the "boys." At Basoko we were robbed, and the authorities instituted a search. I was asked to inspect the boxes of all the workmen on the place. Without warning, every man and boy had to open his trunk, chest, tin box, or other store. I saw young fellows of no more than sixteen or seventeen years who had a dozen pieces of good cloth carefully folded away, watches, jewelry, ornaments, knives, dishes—every kind of white man's tradestuff that could be imagined. When they are thirty those "boys" will be rich men, with women, slaves, and piles of stuff.

The government of the Free State has issued coins for native use. There are large coppers of the value of one, two, five, and ten centimes. There are silver coins of half-franc, franc, two franc, and five franc value. But these coins have no circulation beyond Leopoldville. In the Kasai district and the Upper Congo every commercial transaction is done by barter.

Certain things are so constantly in use as to have fixed values. For articles of trifling value nothing is so good as salt. A standard which varies from place to place is the brass rod, or mitaku. This is simply a piece of brass wire of certain length. The mitaku in the Lower Congo are short, those in the Upper Congo much longer. Beads have ever been used in trade, but the wise traveler avoids them, as their value has dwindled, and the taste not only varies from place to place, but from time to time. The bead which one traveler found useful in a given district may have lost its attractiveness before the next traveler, loaded with a large supply, comes that way.

At Ndombe the brass rod has no vogue. There the cowries (sea shells) are the standard in small transactions. Cowries were once used in many parts of Africa, but in most places have ceased to have value. Ndombe, however, arrogates to himself and family the sole right of wearing brass arm and leg rings. Hence mitaku are not used, and the old-fashioned cowry remains. But the chief tradestuff, of course, is cloth. With it you may buy chickens or goats, pigs or wives. In the Upper Kasai a piece of cloth means eight yards—"four fathoms." In the Upper Congo a piece of cloth is sixteen yards, or eight fathoms. Formerly at Ndombe eight or ten chickens were given for a piece of cloth, value five francs, or one dollar in our currency. To-day one must pay a fathom for each fowl.

The attempt to introduce the use of corn among the natives was unsatisfactory alike to the people and the trader. It has, however, taken hold strongly in the Lower Congo, and in time the use of true money must push its way up the river. Curious is the contempt of all for coppers. Ten centimes in Belgium would give delight to many a boy of twelve or fifteen years. The Congo native frequently throws it away or returns it to the person who gave it to him. Nothing less than a half-franc piece—ten cents—is valued.

I have seen this illustrated many, many times, the first time in my own case. We were visiting a miserable fishing village of poor Bakongo. As I entered the village a naked child, no more than two or three years old, met me. I smiled at him and he at me. I extended my hand, which he clasped and accompanied me for half an hour as I wandered from house to house, never once relaxing his hold upon my fingers. It caused great amusement to the adult portion of the village, as apparently the little one rarely made such friendships. When I was about to leave I took a ten centime piece from my pocket and gave it to him. Such a look of disgust as came over his face would not be expected in any one short of adult years. It was the last time that I gave a copper to a native.

Unquestionably one of the most striking characteristics of the Congo people is loquacity. Their tongues hang loosely, and wag incessantly. Anything will do to talk about. Start one and he will talk until you stop him. Quarrels, troubles, friendships, joys, plans, and achievements, all are retailed at any hour of the day or night. When excited, several will talk together with great vivacity, though it is plain that no one knows what any other is saying.

One of the chief occupations of the man is the palaver. The Portuguese term applies to any serious consultation on any subject, pleasant or otherwise. A palaver may be confined to chiefs or it may include practically all the men of one or more villages. In many towns there is a place for gathering for palavers under a tree known as the palaver tree. Those who participate in a palaver bring their chairs or stools or a roll of skin, which they place upon the ground to sit upon. At the beginning there is more or less formality, and each one presents his view decently and in order; sometimes, however, hubbub ensues, disturbance arises, and the palaver breaks up in disorder. In these palavers frequently speeches of great length and finished oratory are delivered. Not only are the emotions played upon by the speaker, but keen argument is employed, and the appeal is made to the intelligence.

All matters of consequence—tribal, inter-tribal, and dealings with the white man—are settled in palavers. The white man who knows the natives is wise to conform to native customs. If he has some difficulty to settle, some favor to ask, some business to arrange, he will do well to have a formal palaver called in which he himself participates.

On the occasion of my second visit to Ndombe I found the town in great excitement. Going to the chief's headquarters, we found a great palaver in progress. Our coming was looked upon as a favorable omen, and with much formality chairs were brought and placed for us in the midst of the gathering. The remarks were translated to me as they were made.

Ndombe's town is really an aggregation of villages. Not one but four different tribes are represented in the population. The central town, walled and of Bakuba style, was Ndombe's own. Three or four Bakete towns were clustered near it. In another direction were several Baluba towns, and close by them small villages of Batua. These four populations, though living by themselves, were all subject to Ndombe, and the group of villages taken together made a town of some pretension.

The day before our visit, there had been a battle with the Bakete in which several men had been wounded, though none were killed. The trouble was taxes. The state demanded increased payments. The proud Bakuba decided that the Bakete should pay the new tax, and so informed them. Against this there had been a feeling of rebellion, and the Bakete refused to pay the tax. Hence the battle. All were greatly excited. The speeches were full of fire. The men—Bakuba—challenged each other to show mighty deeds of valor; they belittled and derided the unfortunate Bakete; they drew unpleasant contrasts between themselves and their vassals.

Many of the speeches were fine efforts, and the words were emphasized by the most graceful and vigorous gesticulation. Finally an old woman crowded in from one side where she had been listening to the speeches. In impassioned language she described the heavy labors which the women of the tribe already endured. They could stand no more. If the Bakuba were men let them prove it now or forever after remain silent. Force the Bakete to work. Put no more heavy tasks upon your mothers, wives, and sisters. The old woman's speech stirred the audience, and the meeting broke up, the men hurrying to prepare themselves for a new battle.

The market was among the most important institutions of the Congo native. It retains importance to the present day. In the Lower Congo a week consisted of four days, and market was held at each market-place once a week. The markets were named from the day of the week on which they were held. Thus, a Nsona market was a market held on the day of that name.

To these markets people came in numbers from all the country round, and it was no uncommon thing to see thousands thus gathered. There were special places for certain products. Thus, women who brought pottery for sale occupied a set place; those who brought bananas would be grouped together in their section; sellers of camwood, sweet potatoes, kwanga (native cassava bread), palm wine, oil, salt, fowls, pigs, goats—all occupied places well known to the frequenters of the market. In the olden times, of course, there was a section devoted to the sale of slaves.

Such a market presented a scene of active life and movement. Yet order was preserved. No crime was considered more serious than the disturbance of a market. Such an act deserved severest punishment, and those in whose hands the maintenance of order lay never hesitated to kill the offender at once, and to make a public display of his punishment as a warning to all.

There is no question that the Congo native is cruel, and this cruelty shows itself in many ways. The killing of slaves was extremely common. It is true that it was never carried to the extreme in Congoland that it reached in some true negro kingdoms, as Dahomey and Benin. It was, however, customary to kill slaves on the occasion of the death of a man of any consequence. The body of one of the slaves thus killed was placed first in the grave to serve as a pillow for the dead man. It was a common practice to preserve the skulls of victims sacrificed on such occasions as memorials.

Not only were slaves sacrificed to grace the funeral ceremony of chiefs, but often one or more were killed upon occasions of festivity and joy. King Ndombe once presented me a skull. It was that of a Batua slave who had been killed upon the occasion of the chief's coming into power. In this case, apparently, judging by the condition of the skull, the victim had been killed by simply knocking in his head.

Until lately all through the Congo public executions were of a more formal character than this. At Lake Mantumba we were shown the exact mode of procedure. A sort of stool or seat was set upon the ground and sticks were tightly driven in around it, in such a way as to limit the motions of the victim after he was seated; in fact, to almost prevent all movement. A sapling was then thrust in the ground. A sort of cage or framework made of pliant branches was fixed about the head of the victim. The sapling was then bent over in an arch and firmly fastened to the cage, thus holding the head firmly and stretching the neck tense and hard. The hands were tied together, as were the feet. When all was ready the executioner with his great knife at a single blow struck off the head.

Enemies killed in battle were often mutilated, and fingers, nails, bones, or the skulls were treasured as trophies. When the white men first visited the villages of the Upper Congo there was scarce a house without its ghastly trophy, and the houses of great chiefs displayed baskets filled with skulls.

It is doubtful whether the Congo native has as keen a sense of physical suffering as ourselves. In almost every tribe men and sometimes women, are marked with tribal marks upon the face or body; thus, among the Bangala each member of the tribe bears a projection like a cock's comb running vertically across the forehead from the nose root to the hair line. This excrescence is frequently three-quarters of an inch in breadth and of the same elevation. Its development begins in childhood, when a series of short but deep horizontal lines are cut in the child's forehead; these are irritated to produce swelling; later on they are cut again, and again, and again, until the full development is produced. We should certainly find such an operation painful in the extreme. I have seen women whose entire bodies were masses of raised patterns, produced by cutting and irritating.

When being operated upon the subject usually squats or lies in front of the operator, who sits cross-legged on the ground. The head or other portion of the body which is being cut rests upon the lap or knees of the cutter. No particular pain is shown by the subject, though the cuts are often deep and blood flows copiously. A few minutes after the operation, smeared with fresh oil on the wounds, the scarred person walks about as if nothing had happened.

The first subject that I saw treated for rheumatism was a young woman. She was standing before her house door, while the old woman who was treating her was squatted on the ground before her. In her hand the old woman had a sharp, native razor, and with it she cut lines several inches long and to good depth in the fleshy part of the leg of her standing patient. Not once nor twice, but a dozen times the old woman cut, and rubbed in medicine in the open wounds. The patient gave but little signs of pain. Once or twice she winced as the knife went a little deeper than usual; she held a long staff in her hand, and in the most serious moments of the cutting she clutched it a little the tighter. But there were no groans, no cries, nor tears. I have never seen a white person who could have stood the operation with so little evidence of suffering.

Part of the time that we were in Ndombe's district we had charge of an establishment employing 140 natives, more or less. Among these natives was one Casati. I think he was a Zappo Zap. Originally a man of quickness and intelligence, he had become a complete physical wreck through drink and other forms of dissipation. He boarded with a girl named Tumba. One afternoon they presented themselves before me with a palaver. It was some question in regard to payment and service. Like most Bantu difficulties, its beginning seemed to extend backwards to the world's creation.

I knew Tumba to be a worthy and industrious girl; Casati was a miserable and worthless wretch. I therefore refused to decide the difficulty, stating that the parties interested must wait until the return of the true owner of the establishment, who would decide their question. This was not at all to the satisfaction of Casati, who, merely to show his dissatisfaction, took a sharp knife and cut three big gashes in his own shoulder. It seems plain to me, from this apparent lack of pain under scarring, medical treatment, and self-infliction, that there is a notable difference between the Bantu and ourselves.

BAKUMU AT EASE: STEAMER CHAIRS AND PIPES FOR THREE

III.

January 22, 1907.

NATURALLY, in the Congo there is little need of dress. Before the white man's influence most native men wore nothing but a breech-clout—a long strip of cloth passed between the legs and fastened as a belt around the waist—or else a piece of native cloth made from palm fiber, perhaps a yard in width and long enough to go around the body. This latter garment, technically called a cloth, is still the dress of almost all the workmen and workwomen on white men's places, but European stuff has replaced the old palm cloth.

The women were usually much less clad than the men, but the style of dress varied from tribe to tribe. The Bangala woman wore, and still wears, a girdle at the waist, from which hung a fringe of grass or vegetable fiber reaching to the knees. The women of some Aruwimi tribes wear a simple cord, from which hangs in front a bit of grass cloth no more than three or four inches square. On occasion, the Bakuba woman wears nothing but one string of beads around her waist, from which hang in front several large brass or copper rings. The Ngombe women regularly go naked.

Where white influence has become pronounced every one wears white man's cloth, and many have this cloth made up in form similar to those of the Europeans. After a Bantu has begun to be imbued with white man's ideas he is unhappy until he has a jacket, trousers, and hat. In form and material these are frequently so startling as to cause surprise to the person really accustomed to white men's clothes. Thus, a man may be dressed in loose and flowing trousers made of the most brilliant calicoes in gaudy pattern. He may have a jacket made of a strip of handkerchiefing which never was meant to be used as material for clothes, but to be cut or torn into kerchiefs.

But happiness is not complete for the Bantu in transformation until he has a white man's umbrella. Not that he needs it for rain, because when it rains the Bantu always goes into his house and at once falls into a profound slumber which lasts until the rain is over. It is merely fashion, or for protection against the sun, a thing of which the Bantu really has no need. Two boys who were in our employ at Ndombe accompanied us afterwards as personal servants on our long journey up and down the Congo. When the time came to leave them at Leopoldville we took them to the white man's store and asked them what they wanted as a parting gift. Their selections were eminently characteristic. My companion's boy at once declared his wish for an umbrella, while my own, of a far livelier and more sportive disposition, wished an accordion.

It is a common complaint among the white men that the native is ungrateful. Many and many a time have we listened to such tirades. You will hear them from everybody who has had dealings with the Bantu. The missionary complains of it as bitterly as does the trader or the state official. All of them unite in declaring that gratitude does not exist in native character. This seems to us a baseless claim. The African is the shrewdest of traders. It is true that frequently he lets things go to white men for what seems to us a mere nothing. But he gets what he wants in return for his goods. He enjoys bickering. His first price is always greatly in excess of what he actually expects to receive. He will spend hours in debating the value of his wares.

No one need seriously fear for the outcome to the black man in open trade with whites. The purpose of the white man in visiting him and dealing with him is a mystery to the native mind. He can understand the value of palm oil and ivory, for palm oil and ivory he uses himself. Why rubber and copal should be so precious is beyond his understanding. He but dimly grasps the purpose of the state and of the missionary. On the whole, he lends himself to all alike, and being naturally kind, tries to please all and do what is expected of him. Still, he knows that he is being exploited by the foreigner, and it is but fair that he should exploit in return—a thing at which he is an adept. Why, then, should he be grateful for what is done for him? He naturally believes that missionaries, government officials, and traders all gain some advantage from their dealings with him; it is his duty to gain all he can in return in his dealings with them. And there is no especial ground for thanks. There is no reason for gratitude.

I presume it is true that on one occasion—perhaps it has been true on many—a native who had been carefully and lovingly cared for through a long and trying sickness, when restored wished to know what the missionary was going to give him. He had taken all the bad medicines and all the invalid's slops without complaint, but naturally he expected some sort of compensation at the end. Yet the missionary would quote the incident as an example of ingratitude.

It is common to call black Africans dishonest. Here, again, the judgment is undeserved and arises from miscomprehension. The African knows, as well as we do, what constitutes truth, yet he lies, especially to white folk. He has as clear a knowledge of mine and thine as we, and yet he steals from his employer. The explanation lies in the same idea precisely. He thinks we are constantly getting something from him; he in turn must exploit us. The white man is a stranger. Throughout tribal life the stranger is a menace; he is a being to be plundered because he is a being who plunders.

Among themselves, lying is not commended and truth is appreciated; but to deceive a stranger or a white man is commendable. Native houses are often left for days or weeks, and it would be easy for any one to enter and rob them. Yet robbery among themselves is not common. To steal, however, from a white employer—upon whom the native looks as a being of unlimited and incomprehensible wealth—is no sin. It is unfair to stamp the native either as a liar or a thief because he lies to white men and steals from his employer.

Among the Congo natives wealth has weight. The rich man has authority and power and influence because he is rich. There is a servile, cringing, element in the Bantu character which showed itself as plainly in the old days before the white men came as it does to-day. Cringing, toadying, scheming, marked the daily life. While a man was rich he had respect and friends and power. If reverses came he lost them all. None was so poor to do him reverence. Arrogance was the chief element of the chieftain's stock in trade; servility the chief mark of the slave and poor man. White men who have to do with natives are forced to act decisively. They must inspire fear and respect; kindness is weakness. To permit discourtesy or insolence invites contempt. Perfect justice, firmness, and consistency will give the white men who must deal with natives a respected position which vacillation or mistaken friendliness will never gain.

Emotional to a high degree, the native often passes for affectionate. Affection of a certain kind he no doubt has; many examples come to the mind of personal servants who have almost shown devotion to white masters. On the whole, true affection as we know it, unvarying, consistent, which stands the test of varying circumstances, occurs but seldom. Extremely beautiful and touching, however, is the love which every Bantu has for his mother—a love undoubtedly encouraged and strengthened by the polygamous life. A boy's relation to his father is nothing; his relation to his mother is the closest tie in human life. He is of her blood. Her relatives are his. The nearest male connection which he has is her brother. Toward him the boy shows particular respect, but toward his mother true love. She is far nearer and dearer to him than wife or slaves. Through his boyhood she is his refuge in every kind of trouble; in young manhood she is his adviser and confidant; in manhood he still goes to her in every trouble and with every question. There is but one person in his whole lifetime whom he trusts. She is ever sure to be his friend; she never betrays his interest.

All early white visitors to dark African populations were profoundly impressed with the respect shown to the aged. This was genuine. The old man or woman was the repository of wisdom. The experiences through which they had passed made them wise counselors. Tribal affairs were decided by the old. This trait of native character, constantly mentioned by all the early writers, tends to disappear in all those districts where the white man's influence has spread. Such is ever the case. And it is natural.

The white man's wisdom is a different thing from that of the native. Contact with the white man causes contempt and despisal of the wisdom of the ancients. It is the children who always gain this new wisdom from the whites, and with their eating of the tree of knowledge there comes a loss of all respect for older people. Missionaries in vain will preach the fifth commandment to the children in their schools. The reading, writing, and arithmetic which they learn from books, the new ways and manners and points of view which they gain from contact with their teachers, render all such teaching mere platitudes without vital force. The children educated by white men, must always lose respect and admiration for their parents and the elders of their tribes.

Mentally, the native of the Congo is quick and bright. We have already spoken of his ability in languages and his facility in oratory. He delights in saws and proverbs—condensed wisdom. Hundreds and thousands of such proverbs, often showing great keenness and shrewdness, deep observation and insight, might be quoted. No people with a mass of proverbial philosophy, such as the Bantu and the true negroes have, could be considered stupid. In learning new ways and customs and in imitation of others they are extremely quick and apt. Every white settlement in the Congo has introduced new ways of living, and the black boys who can cook well, do fair tailoring, good laundry work, and personal service of other kinds are surprisingly numerous. Under direction they frequently develop great excellence in work.

In a few years after the establishment of the Free State, the caravan service for transporting freight of every kind from the head of navigation at Matadi to Leopoldville, above the rapids, was admirably developed. The men carried their burdens willingly and uncomplainingly; it was extremely rare that anything was lost or stolen. So, too, they have rapidly adopted military life, and the native soldiers under Belgian training present as great precision, promptness, and grace in executing their maneuvers as many white troops would do.

With both the true negroes and the Bantu, belief in witchcraft was prevalent. Sickness, disease, and death were not natural events. That a man should die in battle or from wounds was understood, but that sickness should cause death was not grasped by the native mind. Sickness and death from sickness were regularly attributed to the evil practices of witches. If a man suffered pains in the head or body, it was because some enemy was introducing a mysterious and harmful object into his system. It was necessary, therefore, to adopt some method of undoing the harm. There were men and women whose business it was to detect the author of witchcraft and to recommend means for saving the victim from his operations. Nothing more serious could happen to a man than to be accused of witchcraft. No matter how rich he was; how high his station; how many or how strong his friends—the accusation of witchcraft was dangerous.

A person accused of witchcraft was usually subjected to an ordeal of poison. It was generally the drinking of a poisoned brew produced by steeping leaves, or barks, or roots in water. If the accused vomited the drink and suffered no serious results, his innocence was demonstrated. If, however, the draft proved fatal, his guilt was clear. It is true that sometimes the witch doctor played false, and, in administering the ordeal, might be influenced by bribes.

This whole matter of witchcraft and the ordeal has been magnified by many writers. It is true that there was constant danger for a progressive man, a rich man, or a great chief. Such men would naturally arouse jealousy and envy, and no doubt accusations were frequently made against them without cause. For my own part, however, I have long believed that the ordeal for witchcraft was not an unmixed evil, and I was more than pleased at hearing a missionary, who has been many years in the Congo, state that, after all, while it was subject to occasional abuse, it tended toward wholesome control of conditions in a community.

It is much the custom for white men to speak of Congo natives as big children. Whenever some custom is particularly unlike our own, they will shrug their shoulders and say: "You see, they are only children." I believe as much in the theory of recapitulation as any one. I believe that the life history of the individual repeats the life history of the race.

I believe that one may truly say that children among ourselves represent the stage of savagery; that youth is barbarous; that adult age is civilization. It is true that children among ourselves present many interesting survivals of the savage attitude. In a certain sense savages are children. I think, however, from the points in native character which I here have touched, that my readers will agree with me that the adult native of the Congo is no child. He is a man, but a man different from ourselves. He represents the end of a development, not the beginning.

IV.

January 23, 1907.

HAVING some of the more marked characteristics of the Bantu in mind, let us consider the conditions and circumstances of the white men in the Congo. There are, of course, but three classes—state officials, traders, and missionaries. Practically, the state officials and the traders are in the same condition; the missionary is so differently circumstanced that he must be considered independently.

Few persons can imagine the trying climate and the serious diseases of the Congo region. It is claimed that Nigeria is worse. It may be, but, if so, I should wish to keep away from Nigeria. Fever, of course, abounds in all the Lower Congo districts. If one escapes it for a time it is so much the worse for him when finally he succumbs to the infliction. It is only malaria, but it is malaria of the most insidious and weakening sort. A man is up and working in the early morning; at noonday he takes to his bed with fever; at night or next morning he may again be at his daily work.

It seems a trifling thing—a disease which often lasts less than a day. But the man is left weak and nerveless. The next attack continues the weakening process. Finally, with blood impoverished and strength exhausted, he dies. Of course, the remedy is quinine. Careful people going into the Congo begin to take their daily dose of this specific at the beginning of their journey, so that they may be fortified against attack before arrival. For the most part the English missionaries take two, three, five, or six grains daily throughout the period of their stay. Some foreigners prefer ten grain doses on the 1st, 11th, and 21st of every month. Few really refuse to take it, and such usually find an early grave.

The disadvantage of this constant dosing with quinine is the danger of the dreaded hæmaturic fever. This dread disease rarely attacks a person until he has been a year in the Congo. It is commonly attributed to the system being loaded up with quinine. The instant that its symptoms develop, the order to cease taking quinine is promptly issued. Among the European population of the Congo, hæmaturic fever is regularly expected to have a fatal issue. It is more than probable that the use of wines, beers, and liquors predisposes the system to a fatal result. Plenty of missionaries die of hæmaturic fever also, but the appearance of the disease among them by no means produces the panic which it does among continentals. Perhaps one in five or six cases dies, two of the remainder flee to Europe, the other three recover. But the disease is no trifling matter, and must be seriously taken.

Few persons realize the frightful effect of the tropical sun in Central Africa. When Jameson came down the river from the ill-fated Yambuya camp, natives on the shore sent a flight of arrows against his paddlers, not knowing that a white man was present with them in the canoe. To show them that such was the case and prevent further attack Jameson stood in his canoe and waved his hat at the assailants. It is unlikely that he had it from his head more than a minute or two, but in that time he was stricken with the fever which a few days later caused his death.

Glave, after spending six years in Africa at the state post of Lukolela, returned in safety to his native land. After some years he revisited the scene of his earlier labors, entering the continent on the east coast and passing in safety to Matadi. While waiting for a steamer he was making a short journey on the river in a canoe. His head was exposed for a mere instant to the sun, and Glave was shortly a dead man.

One who has been on three different occasions in the Congo once remarked to me that he could see no reason for the strange and frightful modes of suicide adopted by Europeans who wished to end their lives. All that would be necessary is to seat oneself upon a chair or stool in the open sunshine for a brief period. Yet the Bantu goes out every day with no hat upon his head, and with no apparent bad results. And when he has the fever one of his quickest means of restoration is to seat himself in the open sunshine. Of course, the Bantu does not have the fever as frequently or as severely as the white man.

The Bantu suffers much, however, from sleeping-sickness. For a long time it was believed that this strange disease was peculiar to the dark populations of Africa. The disease formerly was local, and while frightful in its ravages, was not a serious matter. To-day, however, it is extending up and down the whole length of the main river and throughout the area drained by many of its main tributaries.

In its approach it is slow and insidious. The saddest cases are those where the victim attacked was notably intelligent and quick. The subject becomes at first a little moody, and from time to time has outbursts of petulance and anger out of proportion to the exciting cause. These outbursts become more and more common, and assume the character of true mania, during which the person may attack those around him, even though they are his best and dearest friends. It is frequently necessary to tie him, in order to prevent injury to others. Presently the person is affected with stupor, shows a tendency to sleep, even at his work; this increases until at last he is practically sleeping, or in a comatose condition, all the time. In this latter stage of the disease he loses flesh with great rapidity, and presently is naught but skin and bones. At last death takes him, after he has been useless to himself and others for a long time.

The sleeping-sickness is not confined to the Congo Free State, and at the present time its ravages are felt severely in the British district of Uganda. The disease has been investigated by learned commissions, but no satisfactory treatment, at least for an advanced stage of the trouble, has been yet discovered.

There is a tendency among physicians to connect the transmission of the sleeping-sickness with, the tsetse fly. It is, "of course," a germ disease—such being at the present all the fashion. A medical friend in New York tells me that the Japanese have made recent important investigations of the sickness, and that their line of treatment gives greater promise of success than any other. Latterly the disease has attacked white people, and a number of missionaries have died from it or been furloughed home for treatment.

Whole districts of Bantu have been depopulated. We were shown the site of a Catholic mission until lately highly prosperous; the place has been deserted, all the natives under the influence of the mission having died of the sleeping-sickness.

Malaria, hæmaturia, sun fevers, and sleeping-sickness are the most fearful scourges which the white settler in the Congo faces.

We could, of course, extend the list of strange and dreadful diseases, but have said enough to show that every white man who goes into the Congo country does so at a serious risk. No one is quite immune, and the number who even seem to be so is small. No one is ever quite well, and every one is chronically in a state of physical disorganization.

The climate and the actual diseases are bad enough. They perhaps would lose a portion of their terror if the food supply were adequate, wholesome, and nutritious. Even the missionaries use little native food. The state officer and trader use practically none. The chopbox is an institution of the country. Its simplest expression is found at the trading-post of some company where but a single agent is in residence. Once in three months the steamer of his company brings him his chopbox outfit. There are usually two long wooden boxes, one of which contains a great variety of tinned meats, fish, vegetables, and fruit. I never had the least idea until my African experience how many things were put in tins. The second box contains flour, oil, vinegar, salt, and spices. The quantity is held to be sufficient for the three months. In addition to the actual food supply, there is a quota of wine in demijohns and of gin in square bottles.

No one who has not had the experience can imagine the frightful satiety which comes upon one who has fed for weeks from chopboxes.

It is true that "the boy" does his best to serve a palatable dinner. It is true that sometimes a piece of elephant or hippopotamus, a guinea fowl or grouse, some buffalo or antelope, or fresh fish or fowls are brought in by the natives as gifts or trade. But even with this help the poor company agent has the same food, meal after meal, day after day. Frequently the tinned stuff is old and really unfit for eating; but the quota is none too large for his three months' period. Sometimes the flour or macaroni is moldy, having been soaked through with water in the hold of a leaky steamer. The food is not attractive nor substantial. The state officer, the company agent, in Central Africa, is underfed and badly nourished.

Not only does the white man in the Congo suffer physical disorganization; he also suffers mental disintegration. The memory of white men in the Congo weakens. This is a matter of universal observation, and my attention has been called to it repeatedly. A disinclination to any kind of intellectual activity takes possession of one, and only by the exercise of strong will-power can he accomplish his daily tasks and plan for the work of the future. There is a total lack of stimulus.

When to the weakening effects of fever and other illness, and to the depression caused by innutritious food, we add the influence of constant dread of coming sickness and of native outbreaks, it is no wonder that the white man of the Congo is a nervous and mental wreck. At home, accustomed to wines and spirits at his meals, he finds it difficult to discontinue their use. Beer ought to be completely avoided in the Congo; there is no question of its injurious effect upon the liver. Wine may be taken in the evening, and a very little spirits in the night after dinner, without noticeable bad results. But many of these lonely men pay no attention to wise rules of drinking, and through constant dissipation lay themselves open to disease and death. Nor are they always satisfied with intoxicating drinks. The use of opium in different forms is common. Many a time have company agents or state officials come to me and asked for some remedy from my medicine chest, for sudden and distressing pains. In every case it has been a preparation of opium which they have taken.

V.

January 24, 1907.

WITH physical and mental disorganization there must, of course, be moral disintegration. Even the missionaries in an enlightened country like Japan constantly complain of the depressing influences around them.

Such a complaint, to my mind, is preposterous when applied to Japan, but it is easy to understand with reference to Central Africa. If there is but one agent at the station, he rarely sees another white man. Day after day, and all day long, his constant contact is with the black folk. There is nothing to appeal to his better nature. He must pit himself against the scheming and servile native. He must look out for the interests of the company. He must scheme, browbeat, threaten. Chances for immorality abound.

Constant sight of cruelty begets cruelty. Alone in a population so unlike himself, his only safety rests in his commanding at once fear, respect, obedience. He frequently possesses governmental power. The only white man in a large area of country, he must insist upon the fulfillment of the requirements which are passed down to him from his superiors. There are no white men living who could pass unscathed through such a trial.

The wonder is not that from time to time company agents and governmental officials are encountered who are monsters of cruelty. The wonder is, with the constant sapping of the physical, the mental, and the moral nature, that any decent men are left to treat with natives.

Of course, there are almost no white women in the Congo Free State outside the missions. The director-general at Leopoldville, the railroad station agent at the same point, a commandant at Coquilhatville, and two of the officers at Stanleyville have their wives with them. It is possible that there are some of whom I am ignorant, but it is doubtful if there are a dozen white women of respectability in all the Congo—except, of course, the ladies in the missions. Almost without exception, the other state officials and traders have black women.

These black women of the white man are to be seen wherever the white man himself is seen. A man usually selects his black companion shortly after reaching the Congo and supports her in his own house, where he treats her on the whole with kindness. He considers her an inferior being, but treats her like a doll or toy. She is dressed according to her own fancy and frequently brilliantly and more or less expensively. She rarely forces attention upon herself, but where he goes she goes. If he travels on the steamer, she is there; if he makes a trip through the rubber district, stopping night after night in native towns, she is ever one of the caravan. She is true to him and on the whole, though there has been no marriage, he is true to her.

Frequently, a strong affection appears to spring up between the couple, and the hybrid children resulting from the relation are almost always loved and petted by their white father. Not infrequently, the little ones are taken home to Belgium for education, and are generally received with kindness by their father's parents.

On the steamer which brought us back from Congo were two Belgians, one with a little girl, the other with a boy slightly older. The children were well dressed, well behaved, pretty and attractive. And it was interesting to see the affectionate greeting that was given them by their grandparents on their landing at the dock in Antwerp.

At one post, where we were entertained for several days, the lieutenant had his two little daughters, 3 and 5 years respectively, at the table with him at all meal times, together with the other two white men of the station and his two guests. The little ones were extremely pretty and gentle. At the table it is their custom to sing between the courses. Their father almost worships them. While the children are thus constantly petted in public and appear on all sorts of occasions, the black woman rarely if ever sits with her white man at the table or enters the room where he is laboring or receiving guests.

We have described the condition of a single agent at a station. At many stations there is more than one. At first sight, it would seem as if the lot of the agent who with one or two others is at a station would be far happier than that of the lonely man whom we have pictured.

There are, however, two results of the environment to which we have as yet not alluded. On my return to Brussels, after my visit to the Congo, a state official who has never been in Africa asked me with interest and some evidence of concern whether in my judgment it was true that those in Africa were always a little crazy. I told him that I believed such to be the case, and quoted to him a statement made by an old Afrikander: "We are all a little crazy here; it is the sun. You must not mind it." Men on the slightest provocation will fly into the most dreadful fits of anger. A little cause may bring about catastrophe.

The second curious result suggested is the fact that everything appears much larger, more important, and more serious than it really is. A slight, neglect, or insult of the most trifling character becomes an enormous injury. With this unsettled intellectual condition and this constant tendency to magnify and enlarge an injury, we almost always find where two men or more are associated in Congo stations frightful hostilities and enmity. One would think that the common feeling of loneliness would unite men and cement friendships. On the other hand, every subordinate is plotting against his superior. Cabals are formed; injuries planned and developed.

Of course, we understand that criticism, plotting, undermining occur wherever human beings live. But the thing develops to an extreme among the white men of the Congo. When a man has an outside visitor ready to listen to his complaints he will spend hours in pouring out his woes. The most innocent actions and words on the part of his fellows will be warped and misconstrued; imaginary insults and neglects will be magnified, brooded over, and reiterated.

It would be a mistake to think that the men who go to the Congo are bad. Missionaries assert that the quality of those who come to-day is worse than formerly, which may be true. When the Congo enterprise was first launched, sons of good families, lured by the chance of adventure or pining for novelty, enlisted in the service of the state. Probably the number of such men going to the Congo is lessening.

To-day, when all the terrors of the Congo are well known, when the hardships of that kind of life have been repeated in the hearing of every one, rich men's sons find little that is attractive in the Congo proposition. But I was constantly surprised at the relatively high grade of people in low positions in the Congo state. Most of them are men of fair intelligence; some, of education. Not only Belgians, but Scandinavians, Hollanders, Swiss, and Italians, go to the Congo in numbers. They are not by nature brutal or bad; doubtless they were poor, and it was poverty that led them to enter the Congo service. The term for which they regularly enter is three years. No man from any country, could stand three years of such surrounding influence without showing the effect.

In passing, we may call attention to certain curious facts of observation in connection with the strangers who come to Congo. We might suppose that the Scandinavians would particularly suffer physically in going from their northern latitudes into the tropics. On the contrary, it is precisely the Scandinavians who seem most readily to adapt themselves to their surroundings. Almost all the captains of steamers on the Congo River are Norwegians or Swedes.

A record astonishing and presumably unparalleled is presented by the Finns. On one occasion, I was sitting in a mess-room where it proved that each member of the company spoke a different language—French, Flemish, Swedish, Finnish, Spanish, Dutch, German, and English were all represented. On my expressing interest in there being a Finn present, the gentleman of that nationality stated that he and fifty-four of his companions came to the Congo State six years ago; that they were now ending their second term, and that fifty-one out of the original number were still living. I presume the statement was true, and, if so, it is as I have stated, unparalleled. Another member of the company told me later that the case was far more interesting and striking than I realized, as three out of the four who died were drowned, not meeting their death from disease.

There is a tendency for the population of a nationality to flock into the same line of work in the Congo State. Thus, a large proportion of the Finns in question were engineers upon the steamers. The Italians are largely doctors, and one meets with Italian physicians in every quarter of the country.

I have already stated that those who go to the Congo insist that in Nigeria the climatic conditions are still worse for health. If they are no worse, but just as bad, we should find the same disintegration in physical, mental, and moral ways. It is easy to criticise the lonely white man in Central Africa; to stamp him as brutal, cruel, and wicked. But the Englishman occupying a similar position in Nigeria, or even in Uganda, must present the same dreadful results of his surroundings. I suspect that our American young men, isolated in remote parts of the Philippines, show the same kind of decay. Any nation that insists upon bearing the black man's burden must pay the price.

Belgium is the most densely populated land in Europe. It, if any European country, needs room for expansion. Leopold II. claims that his interest in the Congo from the first has been due to a desire to provide an opportunity for Belgian overflow. I am loath to attribute to that monarch so much sagacity. It is, however, true that as a colony of Belgium, the Congo Free State will ever receive a large number of young men who hope, by serving a term in Congo, to better their condition. They realize the dangers and deprivations, but they expect at the end of their three years to come home with a neat sum of money in their possession; with this they think to establish themselves in business for life. Unfortunately, these bright hopes are rarely realized. They start for home in Europe with the neat little sum of money. For three years, however, they have had no social pleasure, have spent no money.

Arrived in the home land, old friends must be entertained. The theater, the saloon, the dance-hall present attractions. Before he knows it, the man has spent his little hoard in foolish pleasures, and has naught to show for his three years of labor. He hates to return to Congo, but the fact that he has been in Congo stands in the way of his securing steady and normal employment in Belgium. At last, without money and without work, after a bitter struggle, he decides that there is nothing left but another term in Congo. If he was a state employé, he decides that he will better himself by entering into the service of a company; or, if he were in the employ of a company, he thinks another company or the state will better appreciate and pay for his services. It is a fatal assumption. The moment that he presents himself before his would-be employers and speaks proudly of his experience in Congo as a reason for his hiring, suspicion is at once aroused that he must have left his earlier employment under a cloud. He is told to call again, and inquiries are set on foot with his old employer, who, irritated at his employé's desertion, gives as unfavorable report as the case will warrant. On returning at the appointed date, the applicant is either told that his services are not wanted, or is offered wages below what he before received. Angered at this lack of appreciation, he goes back to his old employer and offers his services at the old price. This is refused. And the discouraged seeker for work is compelled frequently to accept, in spite of an experience which would make him more valuable, lower wages than he was accustomed to.

VI.

January 25, 1907.

UNDOUBTEDLY the finest houses in the Congo are those at missions. The grade of living in these mission stations is also of the best. This has led to strange criticism by many travelers. One of the latest to visit the Congo State speaks with surprise, and apparently disapproval, of the English missionaries "living like lords."

Yet it is certain that the missionaries, if any one, should live well. The state official and the company's agent go to the Congo with the expectation of staying but a single term. The English missionary goes there with the purpose, more or less definitely fixed, of spending the remainder of his life in his field of labor. No matter how well he is housed or how good his food, he must meet with plenty of inconvenience and privation. If he is to accomplish anything for those who send him, he should be as comfortable as the circumstances will allow. More than that, the English missionary regularly takes with him his wife, and any white woman is entitled to the best that can be had; it is a poor return for what she must necessarily undergo.

There was, of course, mission work in the kingdom of Congo more than 400 years ago. It had an interesting history, it had its periods of brilliant promise, and apparent great achievement. The work was spent, its effect had almost disappeared, when recent explorations reintroduced the Congo to the world. Stanley's expedition aroused the interest of the whole world.

The missionaries were prompt to see the importance of the new field open for their labors. In 1878 three important events in mission history took place. In February of that year Henry Craven of the Livingstone Inland Mission reached Banana; in the same month, the Catholic church decreed the establishment of the Catholic mission of Central Africa, with what is practically the Congo State as its field of operations. In the same year Bentley, Comber, Crudington, and Hartland, representatives of the Baptist Missionary Society, made a settlement at San Salvador, a little south of the Congo River, which became the center from which extended the most widely developed and influential mission work of all the country.

Since that time the representatives of many other missions have undertaken work within the Congo State—which, of course, in 1878 had not yet been established. Some of these flourished for but a brief time; others have continued. At present there are within the Congo limits missionaries of at least eight different Protestant societies—representing England, America, and Sweden—and Catholic missionaries representing five different organizations.

By far the greatest number of the Protestant missionaries are English, even though they may in some cases be representatives of American boards. They naturally carry with them into their stations the English mode of life, traditions, atmosphere. Though the currency of the Congo Free State is reckoned in francs and centimes, they talk all business and quote all prices in shillings and pence; in making out an account everything is calculated in English money, and it is with a certain air of gentle remonstrance that they will convert the total, at the request of the debtor, into Belgian or Congo currency. Their importations all are English; they take their afternoon tea; they look with mild but sure superiority upon all differing methods around them. Few of them really talk French, the official language of the country; still fewer write it with any ease or correctness.

It would seem as if one of the first requirements of a society sending missionaries into a country where the official language is French and where the vast majority of the officials, with whom the missionary must deal and come into relation, know no English, would be that every candidate for mission work should be a competent French scholar. Otherwise there is danger of constant misunderstanding and difficulty between the mission and the government. No such requirement seems to be made.

Unfortunately, there is a strained relation amounting at times to bitterness between the state officials and the English-speaking missionaries. This feeling is general, and there are curiously many specific exceptions. Thus, there are certain missionaries who, by their immediate neighbors among officials, are highly spoken of; for example, the manner, the ingenuity in devising and planning work, the promptness and energy, of Mr. Joseph Clark at Ikoko, are constant themes of admiring conversation on the part of officers at the Irebu camp, and Mrs. Clark's dress, linguistic ability, and cookery are quoted as models to be attained if possible.

At first I thought these officials were poking fun, but soon became convinced that they were speaking in serious earnest, and that it was not done for effect upon myself was evident from the minute details into which the praisers entered. I found an almost precisely similar condition of things at Lisala camp, near the mission of Upoto, where Mr. Forfeitt's wisdom and knowledge of the natives and Mrs. Forfeitt's grace and charm were frequently referred to. At Stanleyville, also, one heard constant praises of Mr. Millman's scholarship and Mr. Smith's skill in photography.

In all three of these stations, the officials would talk dreadfully of British missionaries in general, but for the local missionary they seemed to feel an actual regard. To a less degree, and tinged, of course, with English condescension, there was frequently expressed a feeling of reciprocal regard from the missionary's side. While the representative of the state on the whole was a frightful creature, merely to be condemned, there were usually some local officers, known personally to the missionary, who presented streaks of excellence.

While it is true that a well-built house, and as good meals as can be prepared within the Congo, operate to keep the missionary in better health of mind and body and morals, yet even he feels the disintegration due to the environment. He lives a fairly normal life. The presence of a wife and woman of culture and refinement in the household is a great blessing. Children, of course, are sent home for education and to escape disease. The result is there are no little ones in the mission homes, but, apart from this serious lack, the influence is helpful and healthful.

The missionaries, probably all of them, are abstainers. There is no question that their refraining from wines and liquors is a physical and mental advantage. In the nature of the case, they are constantly subjected to moral restraints, which are lacking to the state official and the company agent. For all these reasons the missionary stands the country much better than any other group of white men.

A white missionary is rarely if ever the sole representative at a station. With a definite continued work, in its nature inspiring, with congenial companions, and the encouragement of others working in the same cause, his lot is often a happy one. But even the missionary has fever, dies of hæmaturia, or must hasten back to England with incipient sleeping-sickness; he, too, becomes anæmic and nerveless; he becomes irritable and impatient; the slightest provocation upsets him, and he magnifies every little grievance, as do his white neighbors in other lines of work.

On the whole, the missionary is the only white man in the country who seriously learns the language of the natives among whom he works. He devotes himself with eagerness to its acquisition. A newcomer in the country, his first desire is to gain sufficient knowledge of the language to teach and preach to the people in their own tongue. Many of these missionaries have written extended grammars and dictionaries of native languages, and the number of translations of portions of the Bible and of religious teachings into these languages is large.

It is true that the mere stranger is sometimes doubtful as to the reality and thoroughness of the missionary's knowledge of his people's language. He hears the missionary give a distinct order to the native, and, behold, the boy does the precise opposite. This has happened too often for one to be mistaken. The missionary shrugs his shoulders and says in explanation that the blacks are stupid or cuffs the boy for inattention. The fact probably is that the missionary gave a different order from what he thought. The black is really shrewd and quick to grasp the idea which the white man is trying to convey to him.

Whether it is true that the white man often gains sufficient control of the language to make himself completely understood by the natives or not, it is absolutely certain that much of the reading of translations into his own language by the native is pure fiction. At one mission which we visited, it was the custom after breakfast for the houseboys of the mission to come in to family prayers. Each was supplied with a translation to be read in the morning's exercise. The boys, seated on the floor, read brief passages in turn. They might, through mistake, skip a whole line or completely mispronounce a word, indicating a total lack of understanding of the passage read, and yet it was done with the same air of satisfaction that would accompany a task well done. My own boy, Manoeli, used to cover whole sheets of paper with meaningless scrawls in pencil, and with an air of wisdom, which he unquestionably thought deceived me, he would at my request proceed to read line after line, and even page after page, of stuff that had no meaning. And even if I stopped him and turned him back to some earlier point, he would begin and go on as if it really meant something. I was constantly reminded by these boys at prayers of Manoeli's pretended reading of fake writing.

On the Kasai River steamer many of the Baluba boys and girls had books from the Luebo mission. These were mostly elementary reading books. Nothing pleased them better, especially if any one seemed to be paying attention to what they were doing, than for a group of them to gather about one who played the teacher. With an open book before him and a cluster of six or eight about him, looking carefully at the syllables to which he pointed, they would call out in unison the sounds represented. It was done with gusto, with rhythm, almost with dancing. It seemed to show remarkable quickness in recognizing the printed syllables.

After I had seen the thing three or four times I myself took the book in hand and centering the attention of the group upon one syllable to which I pointed, I would start them by pronouncing a syllable several lines below; once started, though distinctly looking at the thing to which I pointed, they would call out the complete list, one after another, in proper order, but never the ones, of course, to which my finger pointed and which they pretended to be reading. In other words, these Baluba boys and girls knew their primer by heart and repeated it like parrots, with no reference to the actual text. I must confess that I have little confidence in the ability of most Congo mission boys and girls to read understandingly the simplest of the books with which they deal.

There are different types of Protestant missions. At Leopoldville there would probably be no mission but for the fact that it is the terminus of the railroad and the place from which the river steamers start. The natives directly reached by its work live for the most part on the mission property, in quarters much like those upon the old plantations of the South. They receive their rations weekly and are paid a monthly wage. Early in the morning the rising bell is sounded and morning prayers take place. Work begins and all are kept busily employed upon the grounds and buildings. Noon hours of rest are given, and at evening work for the day stops. There are various religious services and classes meeting after supper on different evenings of the week. The presence of great numbers of workmen and soldiers of the state at Leopoldville introduces conditions not helpful to mission labor. It is necessary, however, to have a force at hand able to help missionaries going up or coming down the river, transporting their baggage and freight, and doing other service constantly called for at a point of receipt and shipping like Leopoldville.

The mission's work is not confined, however, to the town, and teachers are sent to neighboring villages to teach and conduct classes.

VII.

January 26, 1907.

AT Yakusu great stress is laid upon the work of teaching. The mission property adjoins an important Lokele village. Within easy reach are villages of three or four other tribes. It is an area of rather dense population. Villages in number occur all along the shores of the river for miles downstream. Other villages of inland folk lie behind these. Thousands of people are within easy reach. The mission maintains a liberal force of houseboys for the four houses of missionaries; it has also a corps of excellent workmen, who make brick, do carpentering, build houses, and keep the grounds in order. These are not from the local tribe, but are Basoko from down the river. Children from the immediate village flock to the mission school, but this is only the least significant portion of the work. More than 200 teachers are in the employ of the mission, teaching in village schools throughout the country around. To supply text-books, the mission press at Bolobo turns out editions of four or five thousand copies.

Similar in its plan of sending out native teachers to outlying villages is the great work at Wathen, in the Lower Congo. This was once on the main caravan route from Matadi to Leopoldville. Since the building of the railroad it is completely off of beaten lines of travel, and only one who specifically desires to visit it will see it. The main feature of this work, marking it off from all the other mission work in the Congo State, is a central boarding school for native children, where a definite course for study, extending through several years, is continuously carried on. Boys graduating from this school go out as teachers. And the mission demands that the villages thus supplied shall meet the expense of conducting their schools. This seems to me the best educational experiment in the Congo, and scores of villages throughout the district of the cataracts have self-supporting schools with Wathen boys for teachers.

In the official report of the royal commission of inquiry sent to investigate conditions in the Congo Free State recently, there is found this passage:

> "Often, also, in the regions where evangelical stations are established, the native, instead of going to the magistrate, his rightful protector, adopts the habit, when he thinks he has a grievance against an agent or an executive officer, to confide in the missionary. The latter listens to him, helps him according to his means, and makes himself the echo of all the complaints of a region. Hence, the astounding influence which the missionaries possess in some parts of the territory. It exercises itself not only

among the natives within the purview of their religious propaganda, but over all the villages whose troubles they have listened to. The missionary becomes, for the native of the region, the only representative of equity and justice. He adds to the position resulting from his religious zeal the influence which in the interest of the state itself should be secured to the magistrate."—*Translation.*

It is true that the Congo native carries all his grievances to the missionary. On one occasion, when we had been in Leopoldville but a day or two and had seen but little of native life and customs, we noticed a line of fifty people, some with staves of office showing them to be chiefs or chiefs' representatives, filing in a long line to the mission. They squatted under the palaver-tree, awaiting the attention of the missionary. Their errand was in reference to the local market. Formerly there was a market at Leo, important alike to the people of the town and to the producing natives of the country around. There had been disorders and disturbances; the sellers lost their goods through theft and seizure, and for several years it had been discontinued.

After repeated petitions on the part of the people to the government, Bula Matadi yielded, promised restoration of the market, assigned a place, and put up a building. Though apparently all had been done that they had asked, the people were not satisfied, and this delegation had presented itself to the missionary to ask him to present their complaint and desires. The place selected was not a good one; a different one close by the railroad station and the English traders, was requested. The missionary brought the matter to the attention of the local government, which yielded to the people's suggestion, and gave permission for the opening of the market on the following Sunday in the place of preference.

We became interested in this matter, and on the following Sunday the missionary, my companion, and myself made our way to the spot to see how matters were progressing. A considerable number of sellers had come in with produce, mostly kwanga and other foodstuffs. They were beginning to display these upon the ground. Would-be purchasers were gathered in numbers, and among them crowds of Bangala women from the workmen's camp. The sellers seemed suspicious lest attack might be made upon their wares. Their suspicions were, unfortunately, well founded. For a little time things appeared to go well but at last Bangala women, standing by, swooped down upon the piles of stuff temptingly offered for sale, and seizing handfuls, started to run away. One soldier-policeman, who, a few moments before, seemed to be fully occupied with his duty of guarding the railway station, and several idle men and boys joined in the looting. The thing was done as quickly as if there had been pre-concerted plotting and a given signal.

In an instant all was turmoil. Some of the sellers were hastily packing away in cloths what was left of their stores; others grappled with the thieves, some of whom, however, were making good escape with their plunder. We all three rushed in to help the robbed to stay the thieves, and for a few minutes there was a free-for-all fight. Most of the stolen stuff was retaken, and the angry sellers, with all that was left to them packed away, refused to again open up their stores. The missionary suggested that they should move nearer to the trading-post of the English traders and ensconce themselves behind a fence, buyers being allowed to approach only upon the other side, while we three and the white men from the traders should guard to prevent further attack and thieving. Finally, this scheme was put into operation. One or two soldier-police were summoned, the stores were again opened up, though trading had to stop every now and then to permit of the dispersal of the crowd which thronged around awaiting the opportunity for another attack.

Under these difficulties, in which the missionary and my Mexican companion performed prodigies of valor, the market was conducted with a fair degree of success. I was interested in the further history of this market. Our missionary friend shortly wrote me that things had been reduced to order; that the government had built a market-house and supplied regular guards to maintain order; that the number of sellers had increased, and that purchasers flocked to buy.

But all this brilliant promise came to a sad end. When we again reached Leopoldville the market-house was closed; there were no signs of interest. It seems that Bula Matadi thought the market presented an admirable chance for getting even. One day, when the stock of kwanga and other foodstuffs was exceptionally large, the representatives of the law swooped down upon the sellers, claimed that they were in arrears in payment of their kwanga tax, and seized their stock in trade. The result was that the market died.

Among the laws which in their intention, perhaps, were good, but in their application vicious, is one regarding orphan and abandoned children. In native life, unaffected by white influence, there could be no difficulty regarding such children. If a native child were left without a mother it would at once be taken over by the mother's family. There would be no feeling that it was a burden, and it would suffer no deprivation.

Such a thing as an abandoned child, in strictly native condition, is scarcely conceivable. According to state law, an orphan or abandoned child less than 14 years of age may be turned over by the court to missions for care and education. The mission, of course, is entitled to the child's services through a term of years. Advantage of this law has never been taken by Protestant missions, but Catholic missions have at different times had numbers of children committed to their charge and have used their services in the development of property. A child of 14, the limit of the law's application, is better than a child of 12, because capable of immediate service. A boy of 15, 16, 17, 18, would be still better, but, of course, it is illegal to seize a young fellow of that age and employ him at such labor. Once committed, the child remains in the mission's power until manhood.

There is no question that the missions, taking advantage of this law, many times seize boys who are beyond the age limit and many others who are neither orphans nor abandoned. I myself have seen a young man who could not have been less than 19 or 20 years of age, who was married and a member of the Protestant church, who had been taken by the peres under this law. He was brought before the state authorities and immediately set at liberty.

It is due to this fact, that the native goes constantly to the missionary with his complaints—that he looks upon him as the proper person to represent his cause before the state officials; that the missionary, himself, feels it his duty to bring abuses to the attention of the authorities—that the feeling already mentioned between the missionary and the state official has arisen. There have been, unfortunately, abundant occasions for intervention; there have been flagrant and cruel things which the missionary has felt called upon to report.

I do not doubt the honesty of the missionary. I have sometimes felt, however, that they have become so filled with a complaining spirit that they are incapable of seeing any good. I have heard them for hours complain of things that neither in themselves nor in their results were really open to criticism. I have heard them carp and find fault with any matter with which the name of the government could be connected. If their attention is called to some apparent purpose to reform abuses, they shake their heads and say it will come to nothing; it is a subterfuge. If, as time passes, the thing assumes the appearance of reality, they say there is some hidden and mysterious purpose back of it; the state would never do so well unless it were preparing some new iniquity. The attitude of complaint becomes habitual: the ability to see improvement seems completely lost.

The first time that I attended family prayers in a missionary home I waited with some interest to hear the petition in favor of the government. When it came, it assumed this form: "O Lord, stay the hand of the oppressor. Pity and aid the oppressed and overburdened. Prevent cruelty from destroying its victims. Interfere with the wicked and designing schemes of the oppressor."

A dozen such expressions and petitions were uttered, but no request for divine wisdom and enlightenment for the rulers. It can easily be conceived that, where godly and pious men cherish such sentiments toward representatives of the state, the feelings of state officials toward missionaries are little likely to be completely friendly.

BACHOKO BRINGING IN RUBBER, DJOKO PUNDA

VIII.

January 27, 1907.

THE actors in the Congo drama are now clearly before us—the black man and the white man, the state official, the trader, and the missionary.

Travel in the Congo state is, naturally, for the most part by water. The mighty river is the main member in a water system surpassed only by that of the Amazon. The Congo itself presents a total length of almost 3,000 miles, of which more than 2,000 is navigable. The vast network of tributary streams, with a total length of almost 17,000 miles, gives nearly 5,000 miles more of navigation connected with that of the main river.

To-day these thousands of miles of navigation are utilized by a fleet of steamers eighty or more in number. Most of these are vessels of the state; a smaller number belong to the great concession companies; a few are the property of the missions. Many of them are small, but some of the more recent steamers constructed for the state are vessels of 400 tons burden. They are flat-bottomed steamers of small draft, because the rivers through which they ply are often shoaled by sand banks. Even the mighty Congo itself, at certain seasons of the year, becomes dangerous and almost impassable, even for vessels of this light draft. By means of these boats it is easy now for travelers not only to go over the chief part of the main river but to enter the larger tributaries at their mouth and travel for hundreds of miles up towards their sources.

It can be well imagined with what surprise the natives saw the first steamer. The pioneer vessels were brought in pieces to the head of navigation for sea steamers, and then transported by human carriers the weary distance from Vivi, near Matadi, around the cataracts to Stanley Pool, where the parts were assembled and the vessels prepared for service. Some of the earliest steamers are still in service, and, while they have been eclipsed in size and power and speed by later vessels, have a true historic interest. No vessel on the Congo deserves more or has a better record than the Peace. This was the earliest of the mission steamers, presented to the B. M. S. by Robert Arthington of Leeds, England. It was throughout its history in charge of George Grenfell, the intrepid missionary explorer, whose death took place during our stay in the Congo.

We saw the little vessel at Yakusu, and looked at it with especial interest. In it George Grenfell explored many thousand miles of unknown waterway. With it he made the study which enabled him to construct the best navigation maps and charts so far published of the Congo—charts which the state still uses on its own steamers.

The state steamers are, of course, primarily for the service of the state. So far as the main river is concerned, a steamer is started from Leopoldville for the trip to Stanley Falls every ten days, taking from twenty-four to thirty days to make the journey. The down trip requires less time, and can be made under favorable circumstances in fourteen days—the usual time being seventeen or more. By these steamers state officials are taken to their posts, workmen and soldiers are transported to their place of service, chopboxes and other supplies are taken to the state employés, materials for construction are taken to the place where needed, products, such as rubber, ivory, and copal, are brought to Leopoldville for shipment. Generally they are well loaded with both passengers and cargo.

The company boats do for the company what state boats do for the state—transporting from place to place, bringing in supplies, taking out products. Similarly the mission steamers are intended solely for the movement of the missionaries and their supplies. The state boats may carry freight and passengers, but only when they are not loaded fully with the materials of the state. Arrangements must be made by strangers, and it is only when the state is favorable that they may travel or ship goods. The company boats are not allowed to carry outside passengers or freight without the express permission of the state, but are obliged to carry state people and freight in cases of especial need. If a mission steamer carries outside passengers or freight, it can do it only gratuitously.

In the steamers of the state the traveler who has permission to embark upon them pays for a ticket, which entitles him merely to transportation; he is expected to pay five francs a night additional for his cabin; for food he pays twelve francs per day during the period of the voyage. The steamers of every class tie up at evening, and no traveling is done at night. In steamers of the larger class there may be as many as four white employés—the captain, his assistant, a commissaire, or steward, and the engineer. In smaller steamers there are only the captain and the engineer. All the crew and employés in the cabins, mess, and deck are blacks. In steamers with an upper deck, the blacks are expected to stay below; only when called for special service are they allowed on deck.

No black man remains on board during the night. Even the personal servants, or boys, of the white passengers must go with the crew and other workmen on to shore to spend the night. As promptly as the ship is fastened, the black men, women, and children, with cooking utensils, food supplies, bedding, and beds, hasten off on to shore to pick out the spot on the bank, or in the forest, where they will spend the night. It is an animated and curious scene. As darkness comes on, the fires for cooking their evening food have been kindled here and there over the terrace or in the forest, and the groups gathered around them while the cooking proceeds, or eating takes place, are picturesque in the extreme. At daybreak the steamer whistles the signal for all on board, and the whole mob come rushing—for no time is lost, and it is easy to be left behind in the forest—pellmell on board.

The fuel for the steamers is wood, cut from the forest. One of the most serious problems which the state has had to face is the securing of sufficient and continuous fuel supply. Wood-posts have been established wherever possible; the natives at the wood-posts are required to supply, in form of tax, for which a small compensation is, however, returned, a certain number of yards or fathoms of wood. A space is marked out on the ground as many yards in length as there are cutters of wood. Stakes are placed at intervals of a yard and ropes are stretched from one to another at a yard's height. Each bringer of wood is expected to fill the space indicated for him to supply. Much time is lost, even under the best circumstances, in taking wood at these wood-posts. Whenever possible, the night's landing is made at a wood-post, and as large a supply of fuel as possible is brought on board during the night. Sometimes it happens that several steamers reach a wood-post in quick succession before a new supply has been procured; under such circumstances the crew frequently must cut wood for itself in the forest, a task which they greatly dislike.

In each crew is a capita or head man, whose business it is to oversee the work and to assign the portions of the task. He is held responsible for the service of his subordinates, and usually is more successful in securing prompt, efficient service than a white man would be. He is himself, of course, frequently watched and directed by a white officer, but on the whole he is the one man on the vessel who comes into direct contact with the black laborers.

It is extremely interesting to watch the black hands on a steamer when for any reason landing is made at villages. Many of them have bought a stock in trade at Leopoldville. Beads, pieces of bright cloth, salt, accordions, made-up clothes, hats, umbrellas—these are the things they are most likely to have brought with them. A crowd of women and children always flocks to the landing, and quickly the bartering begins. If the steamer-boy has had experience, he makes money both coming and going. All the product of his sales en route between Leo and Stanley Falls he at once invests in rice when he reaches the district in which it is so largely produced. This forms his capital upon his return to Leopoldville, where it brings a price largely in excess of what it cost him and enables him to stock up again for new business on his next voyage.

Our first long voyage on these river steamers was the journey from Leopoldville to Wissmann Falls, on the High Kasai. We were in a steamer of the Kasai company, and we had hard luck in wood-posts, frequently arriving when earlier steamers had taken all the fuel. We were forced repeatedly to tie up for the night close by the forest and to drive our force of cutters into the dense, almost impenetrable, mass of trees, bound together by hundreds and thousands of creeping plants and vines. The natives not only do not enjoy the cutting of the wood; but they do not like to be turned out into the dense forest for sleeping. Particularly after a heavy rain, conditions are disagreeable for sleeping. Many a time it seemed hard to force them to pass the night in such conditions, on the wet ground, under the dripping foliage, in haunts of mosquitos and other insects.

While we were in the Kasai country the governor-general made his journey of inspection throughout the upper Congo. When we reached that district in our later journey we found that he had ordered a most excellent reform, which had been carried out. The steamers were put under orders to stop at wood-posts or at villages every night, tying up against the forest only on those rare occasions, when it was unavoidable. The order also provided for the immediate erection at all wood-posts and villages of a great hangar for the shelter of the black people. A hangar is a substantial roof, supported on posts, for giving shelter at night or in rainy weather. These hangars for the shelter of the black people from the steamers are enormous things, capable of sheltering 150 to 200 people and giving ample opportunity for the building, by each little group, of its own fire for cooking and for warmth. While the natural travel in the Congo Free State is by boat upon the river, there is, of course, land travel as well.

There are almost no beasts of burden in the country. Horses seem to lose all force and vigor; oxen suffer in many districts from the tsetse fly. The State has made several interesting experiments in its effort to secure some animal of burden. Indian elephants have been brought into the country, partly with the view of using them as carriers and partly in the hope that they might be used in the domestication of the African elephant. At present, of course, the latter animal has the reputation of being untamable, though for several hundred years in history we know that it was tamed and used on a large scale for draft and war. The experiments so far made toward its recent domestication have not met with much result. Camels have been introduced as an experiment, and in Leopoldville one sees a little cluster of them under an imported Arab driver.

In the district where the zebra is at home, efforts are being made now to tame that animal and use it for practical purposes. But notwithstanding all these interesting experiments, some of which ultimately may be successful, it must be stated that at present there is absolutely no beast of burden in the Congo. The result is that land travel must be done by caravan. The outfit of the traveler, his trade stuffs, and whatever else he may have for transportation, must be carried on human backs.

With the exception of a few experimental roads built with reference to the introduction of automobiles for moving freight, there is nothing which we would call a road in all the Congo. The native, on the march, always go in single file. The trails leading from village to village are only a few inches wide, though they are usually well worn, sometimes to a depth of several inches into the soil. Most of them are in use so constantly that there is little or no grass growing in them. For my own part, when they are dry I could ask no better path for travel, and my ideal of African travel is the foot journey over the native trails.

Many white men do not like to walk, and must have their hammock. It is a simple hammock, usually made of a strip of foreign stuff swung by ropes to a long bamboo or palm pole. Unless the person to be carried is extraordinarily heavy, there will be two or four carriers. When four men are carrying a hammock, two in front and two behind shoulder the pole at its two ends. Usually the carriers swing along at a sort of dog trot. Frequently they strike their palms against the carrying pole to make a noise, and indulge in an explosive snort in taking breath. They may sing or shout or cry when carrying, and if they approach a settlement, either native or foreign, their pace quickens, their exertion increases, they cry and yell with great force, increasing their noise and outcry with the importance of the person carried. When they rush up to the place where he is expected to dismount, the whole party bursts into a loud yell, which would appall the bravest if he never had heard it before, as they stop suddenly.

For my own part, I can imagine nothing more disagreeable than traveling in a hammock. The four men rarely are on the same level, and the jolting and movement up and down, now of one's head and upper body, now of one's feet tilted high in air, are extremely disagreeable; from one's position he must look up constantly into the sky and see nothing of the country through which he travels; if the sun shines, his face must be shaded, and if one wears, as he usually must do, his cork helmet, it is difficult to adjust it in any way other than putting it over the face. Personally, I invariably have a half-day of fever after a hammock journey. I would rather walk thirty miles every day than to go twenty in a hammock.

There are still opportunities in the Congo for making fine journeys on foot. From Stanley Falls to the English steamer on the Lake is a foot journey of forty days over a good road. If I had had the time, I should have made that journey.

There are at present two operating railroads in the Congo Free State, besides a little line of a few miles running from Boma into the country back. The more important of these two roads is the Congo Railroad, running from Matadi to Leopoldville. Before its building it took freight three weeks to go by caravan around the cataracts. The engineering difficulties of this line were all in its early course within a few miles of Matadi. Several years were spent in the construction of the road, which has a total length of about 250 miles. It is a narrow-gauge road, well-built, and fairly equipped. After a train once starts it is entirely in the hands of black men as no white conductor or engineer is employed in its running.

Two classes of cars are run, one for whites, first-class, the other for blacks. The fare for first-class passage from Matadi to Leopoldville at the time we made the journey was 200 francs, or $40; the second-class, jimcrow-car fare, was 40 francs, or $8. The journey requires two days for its accomplishment. Starting from Matadi at 7 in the morning, the train reaches Thysville at 5 or 6 in the evening, and stays there for the night. Starting at 7 the next morning, it is expected to reach Leopoldville at 2 o'clock in the afternoon, but usually is from half an hour to two hours behind time. The road, during the period of its construction, was often considered a wild speculation, but it has paid remarkably well, and its stock sells at an advance of many hundreds per cent upon face value.

The second serious obstacle to Congo navigation—the Stanley Falls—is got around in a similar way by a railroad line just finished. This line of railroad from Stanleyville to Ponthierville, is about 75 miles in length. It has just been finished and at the time of our visit, while it was transporting passengers on account of the state, was not open to general travel. We had the pleasure, however, of going the full length of the line, a journey which required some eight hours. The whole course of the railroad is included in dense forest, and nothing is to be seen in all the journey except the forest. There is no question that this little piece of tracking will have great business importance. Hundreds of miles of navigable water lie above Ponthierville, and steamers—both state and railroad—are already plying upon it. A country of great resources is by it brought into near relations with that portion of the Congo already developed. This piece of road forms but a small part of the line planned, which is known by the name of the Great Lakes railroad. Construction is in progress upon another section of it.

While we made our journey from Stanleyville to Ponthierville by rail, we made the return journey by canoe, in order to see the rapids. Of course, the construction of the railroad had already affected this old route and mode of travel. Until lately all passengers and freight going up the Congo beyond Stanleyville were forced to make the journey by canoe.

It is the district of the Congo where the canoe reaches its fullest development and most striking expression. There are canoes cut from a single tree-trunk which will carry tons of freight and scores of men. Some of the great native chiefs had canoes of state in which they were paddled from place to place by a hundred or more paddlers. While the one in which we made our journey was by no means so pretentious, it was certainly large enough for all practical purposes. An awning, or rather a thatched roofing, extended over the middle third of its length to protect us and our things from the sun. An officer of the state, an Italian, accompanied us through half our journey to see that we met with prompt and proper treatment. And two native soldiers were deputed to accompany us the total distance and to take the canoe in charge when we finally reached the landing at Stanley Falls. It was a most interesting experience, for nothing that I had read had prepared me for so well developed a system.

When we came to the rapids we and our stuff were landed. The signal had been given as we approached the beach, and by the time that we were ready to take the trail around the rapids the women of the native village had presented themselves with carrying straps, ready to move our freight. In ten minutes time everything was ready and the caravan upon its way, twenty or thirty women carrying our boxes, satchels, provisions, and collections. Meantime, our paddlers were occupied in passing the canoe down through the rapids, and by the time we reached the lower beach they were there ready for re-embarkation. We took five days for our journey, though it might have been done in half that time or even less.

At each village where we landed we found arrangements for the traveler. A neat house of two or three rooms, constructed by the state, was at our disposition. It was supplied with table, chairs, and beds. Near the house for white travelers was a comfortable hangar for blacks, and near it a large hangar for the storage of freight and baggage. The paddlers who started with us at Ponthierville were dismissed after a day of service and a new set of paddlers taken on, furnished by the village chief. These, after a few hours of service, were again at liberty, and a new crew supplied. Everything was done with promptitude and readiness. The journey was one of the most interesting I ever made.

You understand, of course, that all this service, the carrying of freight around the rapids by the women of the village and the supplying of male paddlers by the chief were taxes to the state, for which a nominal return in money or trade goods is allowed. At no point did we see the slightest evidence of difficulty in furnishing the service or of dissatisfaction in supplying it. Everywhere the people seemed to take it as a pleasant thing. It is entirely possible that when the caravan service was at its height and all freighting and traveling was done upon the river, it may have been a heavier burden. But nowhere did the people seem to show fear, hostility, or the effects of bad treatment. If we had made the long walking trip above referred to, from Stanleyville to the Lake, we would have found analogous arrangements for the traveler's comfort. Good sleeping-houses, with necessary furniture, occur at intervals of four or five hours throughout the entire journey, and no one need sleep out of doors a single night, unless he chooses to do so.

It will be seen that one to-day may go easily throughout the enormous area of the Congo Free State without serious hardship and really with much comfort. But, as a matter of fact, there are almost no true travelers in the area. One can hardly call a state official, on his way to his post, or going from place to place in the performance of his duty, a traveler. Nor is a company agent, making his tour for the collection of rubber, or for inspection of property, exactly one's ideal of a traveler. Nor is the missionary, coming back from furlough or going home invalided, a traveler. The number of actual travelers in the Congo at any time is small. My photographer and myself, I think, might be called travelers.

We spent fifty-three weeks in the Congo Free State. During the period of time that we were there we learned that Mr. A. Henry Savage-Landor spent a few days in the High Ubangi. He came in from the north, visited only one station of a company, and then went out again. Mr. Harrison, who, some little time ago, took a group of pygmies from the High Ituri forest to London, was again in the country, though he had left his little people behind him.

At the same time, an English gentleman was hunting the okapi (that curious antelope) in the same district. When we were coming out and were delayed at Leopoldville, a Capt. Daniels of the English navy arrived at Leopoldville, having made his way across the continent from the east coast. At Bolengi we met a Mr. Creighton, an American clergyman, who had made the way so far from Mombasa. Mr. Verner, bringing back his native group from the St. Louis exposition, was in the Congo during the same period.

On the steamer coming down from Stanley Falls, we had for fellow passengers, M. and Mme. Cabra. M. Cabra was a royal commissioner, having been sent to the country by Leopold himself, to make a careful examination of conditions throughout the whole upper region of the Ituri and Congo rivers. M. and Mme. Cabra entered Africa at Mombasa; they had traversed on foot the forty days of journey I have referred to, but as the purposes of their investigation required them to zigzag back and forth instead of following a direct path, they had occupied a much longer period of time and covered much more distance. Eighteen months on their long journey, they both of them reached Matadi in good health, and Mme. Cabra is probably the first lady to have crossed the African continent in the equatorial regions from ocean to ocean.

Now, these were the only travelers besides one Frenchman, who was a mystery, of whom we heard or whom we met in our fifty-three weeks in Congo experience. It is unlikely that there were many others. The stranger in the Congo is talked of everywhere. We were not within hundreds of miles of Henry Savage-Landor, or Mr. Harrison, or the okapi hunter, but we heard of their existence. Even if the given list is but the half of Congo travelers during the year, it can be seen that the real traveler is a rarity within the limits of the state.

IX.

January 28, 1907.

IN the romantic history of African exploration and development there is no more interesting chapter than that relating to the Congo. In 1854 Livingstone finished a great journey into the continent; in it he had visited a portion of the district drained by the Kasai River. In his final journey we find him again within the district of what to-day forms the Congo Free State; he discovered Lake Moero in 1867 and Lake Bangwelo in 1868; he visited the southern portion of Tanganika in 1869, and followed the course of the Congo to Nyangwe.

At that time no one knew, few if any suspected, that the river he was following had connection with the Congo. Livingstone himself believed that it formed the uppermost part of the Nile, and in all the district where he saw it, its course from south to north would naturally lead to that opinion. It was his heart's desire to trace the further course and determine whether it were really the Nile or a part of some other great river. Death prevented his answering the question.

Backed by the New York *Herald* and the *Daily Telegraph*, Stanley, on November 17, 1874, struck inland from the eastern coast of Africa, with the purpose of determining the question as to the final course of the great river flowing northward, discovered by his missionary predecessor. He circumnavigated Lake Victoria, discovered Lake Albert Edward, and made the first complete examination of the shore of Tanganika. He reached the Lualaba—Livingstone's north-flowing stream,—and, embarking on its waters, devoted himself to following it to its ending.

There is no need of recalling the interesting experiences and adventures of his journey; every one has read his narrative. Suffice it to say that his great river presently turned westward so far north of the Congo mouth that one would never dream of connecting the two waters, but as unexpectedly it turned again toward the southwest and finally showed itself to be the Congo. During the interval between Stanley's two great expeditions—the one in which he found Livingstone and the one in which he demonstrated the identity of the Lualaba and the Congo—there had been a growing interest in Europe in everything pertaining to the Dark Continent.

This interest, which was widely spread, was focused into definite action by Leopold II., king of the Belgians, who invited the most notable explorers of Africa, the presidents of the great geographical societies, politicians, and philanthropists, who were interested in the progress and development of Africa, to a geographic conference to be held in Brussels. The gathering took place in September, 1876, at the king's palace. Germany, Austria, Belgium, France, Great Britain, Italy, and Russia were represented. The thirty-seven members who made up the conference represented the best of European thought.

From this conference there developed the International African Association. This Association organized a series of local national associations, through which the different countries interested should conduct investigations and explorations in Africa upon a uniform plan, and with reference to the same ideas and purposes. It possessed, also, a governing international commission, of which the king of the Belgians was the president, and upon which were representatives of Germany, and France, and the United States, Minister Sanford replacing a British representative. This committee laid out a definite plan of exploration. Its first expedition was to go in from the east coast at Zanzibar, passing to Tanganika. The commission adopted as the flag of the International African Association a ground of blue upon which shone a single star of gold.

The Association's plan included the discovery of the best routes into the interior of Africa; the establishment of posts where investigators and explorers could not only make headquarters but from which they might draw supplies needed for their journey. These advantages were to be extended to any traveler. The expeditions themselves were national in character, being left to the initiative of the local national committees which had been developed by the Association. This Association existed from 1876 to 1884. During that time six Belgian, one German, and two French expeditions were organized, accomplishing results of importance.

It was in November, 1877, that the result of Stanley's expedition came to the knowledge of the world. It wrought a revolution in the views regarding Central Africa. In Belgium it produced at once a radical change of plan. The idea of entering the heart of Africa from Zanzibar was abandoned. The future operations of the A. I. A.—at least, so far as Belgium was concerned— would extend themselves from the Congo mouth up through the vast river system which Stanley had made known. Details of this mode of procedure were so promptly developed that when Stanley reached Marseilles in January, 1878, he found an urgent invitation from the king of the Belgians to come to Brussels for the discussion of plans of conference.

After a full study of the matter, it was determined by the Belgian committee that a society should be organized with the title of the Committee of Studies of the High Congo. This, it will be understood, was purely a Belgian enterprise. It had for its purpose the occupation and exploitation of the whole Congo district. For this purpose prompt action was necessary. In February, 1879, Stanley went to Zanzibar and collected a body of workmen and carriers. With this force of helpers and a number of white subordinates he entered the Congo with a little fleet of five steamers, bearing the flag of the A. I. A. Arrived at Vivi, where he established a central station, he arranged for the transportation of his steamers in sections by human carriers to the Stanley Pool above the rapids.

He worked with feverish haste. France was pressing her work of exploration, and there was danger of her seizing much of the coveted territory. Portugal, too, was showing a renewed interest and activity, and might prove a dangerous rival in the new plans. Native chiefs were visited and influenced to form treaties giving up their rights of rulership in their own territories to the Association. Lands were secured for the erection of stations; the whole river was traversed from Stanley Pool to Stanley Falls, for the purpose of making these treaties and securing the best points for locating the stations. The Committee of Studies of the High Congo now possessed at least treaty rights over a vast area of country, and by them governmental powers over vast multitudes of people. It had these rights, it had a flag, but it was not yet a government, and it stood in constant danger of difficulties with governments. About this time it changed its name from the Committee of Studies of the High Congo to the International Association of the Congo.

Meantime events were taking place which threatened the existence of the Association. Portugal began to assert claims and rights which had long been in abeyance. She proposed to organize the territory at the Congo mouth, and which, of course, was of the greatest importance to the Association, into a governmental district and assume its administration. In this project she found willing assistance on the part of England.

Never particularly enthusiastic over the scheme of Leopold II., England had shown no interest at all during the later part of all these movements. It is true that she was represented at the first conference held at Brussels; it will be remembered that in the later organization an American had replaced the English representative. No work had been done of any consequence by a British committee. No expedition had been sent out. By the treaty with Portugal, England would at one stroke render the whole Congo practically worthless. The crisis had come. France and Germany came to King Leopold's help. The former recognized the political activity and status of the Association and promised to respect its doings; Germany protested vigorously against the Anglo-Portuguese treaty, which fell through.

Bismarck, who favored the plans of the Belgian monarch in Africa, officially recognized, on November 3, 1884, the Association as a sovereign power, and invited representatives of the powers to Berlin for the purpose of establishing an international agreement upon the following points: First, commercial freedom in the basin of the Congo and its tributaries; second, application to the Congo and the Niger of the principle of freedom of navigation; third, the definition of the formalities to be observed in order that new occupations of African shores should be considered as effective. The conference began November 15th, Bismarck himself presiding. Fifteen powers participated— Germany, Austria, Belgium, Denmark, Spain, United States, France, Great Britain, Italy, The Netherlands, Portugal, Russia, Sweden, Norway, and Turkey.

As the result of three months of deliberation, the Congo State was added to the list of independent nations, with King Leopold II. as its ruler. Promptly the new power was recognized by the different nations of the world.

CHILDREN AT MOGANDJA, ARUWIMI RIVER

X.

January 29, 1907.

WHAT has the Congo Free State done during its twenty-two years—almost—of existence?

It has taken possession of a vast area of land, 800,000 square miles in extent, and dominated it. It has most skillfully developed a mighty waterway. We are already familiar with the simple and original method of development which has been and is being pursued. We have already called attention to the fact that, notwithstanding interruption to navigation here and there in the Congo and its larger tributaries, there are long stretches of navigable water above the obstacles. The plan of utilization and development has been to occupy directly the natural stretches of navigable water and to get around the cataracts by the shortest railroad lines possible. This has been done already at two points, and will be done at others in the near future. It is the most economical manner of developing a way of penetration into the great area to be developed and exploited.

It has continuously carried on geographical explorations by which the world's knowledge of African geography has been profoundly increased. We have already called attention to the fact that during the eight years when the A. I. A. was in existence, Belgium equipped and maintained six expeditions; during the same period France maintained but two, Germany one, and England none. In other words, Belgium did more for geographic science during that time than the other three great nations combined.

It has put an end to inter-tribal wars, to execution of slaves at funerals and festal occasions, and to cannibalism in all those districts to which its actual authority extends. It is understood, of course, that twenty years is a short time for the penetration of the state's authority into remote parts of its territory. There are still inter-tribal wars in remote parts of the Congo Free State; executions and the eating of human flesh are no doubt still common in districts which have but little felt the influence of the white ruler. With the extension of the definite power of the state into these remoter sections, these evils will disappear as they have disappeared in the more accessible portions of the country.

It has developed a native army which is available in case of attack upon the integrity of the state, and which serves as a policing party within its territory. In the first days of the state's history its soldiery was drawn from the Zanzibar district, and to a less degree from the English possessions along the western coast of Africa. It soon was realized that from every point of view this condition was undesirable. Between the foreign soldiery and the native people there were no bonds of common interest. No national feeling or spirit could develop among them. From the point of view of expense the foreign soldier was extremely costly. For these different reasons the state early developed the idea of an army made of Congo natives. To-day there are but few foreign soldiers in the public force.

If there is ever to be a real nation in the Congo district there must develop in some way a feeling of unity of blood and interests among the people. In tribal life each tribe is absorbed in its own interests—petty, of course—and looks upon all other tribes as enemies. Many of the tribes were insignificant in number and in the area which they occupied. Nothing but an outside influence can unite into one useful whole such a multitude of petty, distrustful, hostile groups of men. In the public force there are soldiers from almost every tribe within the Congo. At the great training camps men are brought together who speak different languages, have different customs, and come from widely separated areas. Under the military discipline, these men are brought into close and long continued relations. They must accommodate themselves to one another. They must respect each other's ways of thought and doing. At the end of his term of service the soldier goes out necessarily broadened in his ideas, necessarily less prejudiced and more tolerant. The army is the most important influence toward arousing national existence.

It has conducted many interesting experiments and researches along scientific lines. While these had frequently practical ends, they were in themselves worth doing, and their beneficent results are not confined to the Congo. Thus, at Leopoldville there is a well-equipped bacteriological institute for the study of tropical diseases. Naturally, the most of its attention up to the present has been given to the subject of sleeping-sickness.

The experiments upon the utilization of the African elephant and the zebra have general interest; if they fail, the warning may be useful; if they succeed, their results will be by no means confined to the Congo Free State. At Eala is a botanical garden creditably devised and well conducted. Six hundred species of plants are there in cultivation, something more than half of them being foreign species. There experiments are being made upon a broad scale to discover the uses of native plants and the possibility of cultivating them to advantage. Forty species of African plants yield rubber; those the product of which is of a quality to warrant experimenting, are here being cultivated with reference to ascertaining their value in plantations. Foreign rubber producers, coffees from different portions of the globe, medicinal plants, dye and other useful plants are being tested to find out how they flourish in Congo.

Nor is the interest of the Congo Free State in scientific investigations limited to its own enterprises. Some time ago a British commission, consisting of three specialists in tropical medicines, visited the Congo with the purpose of investigating the sleeping-sickness. Not only were they given every facility for their investigation, but after they returned to England the total expenses of their expedition were returned with the compliments of the State government in recognition of the general value and utility of their investigations. Individual investigators and expeditions of a scientific character within the Congo State always have found the government interested in furthering and aiding their studies.

It has developed a significant and growing section of the world's commerce. When Stanley came down the Congo, the value of the exports from that region was so small that it might be neglected. To-day the Congo furnishes the world with ivory and supplies a most significant portion of the rubber which is used. To-day Antwerp is the greatest market for these two products. That Liverpool should lose in relative importance in the matter of West African trade is no doubt hard for Englishmen. But the world gains by having several great trading centers in place of one.

It has checked the extension of the Arab influence with all its horrors. To one who reads Stanley's description this means much. With this checking, the foreign slave trade ceased. Do not misunderstand me. There was much admirable in the Arab culture. There is no question that the practical men, whose views we always keep in mind, and to whom we make our argument, would approve the substitution of it or the barbarism that existed before. But it is certain that it stood in the way of European influence; that it came into conflict with European ideas, and if it were desirable that these should ultimately prevail, the Arab life and culture must disappear.

We might, of course, continue and extend our list of the achievements of the Congo Free State. We have said enough, however, to show that it has done much toward carrying out its promise to civilize and modify the native population in the direction of our own ideals. Even the bitter enemies of the Free State government will admit all this, and more. But they claim that all the credit of it disappears in view of the atrocities, the cruelties, and horrors connected with its own administration.

Atrocities no doubt exist; they have existed; they will exist. They are ever present in cases where a population of natives is exploited by an active and aggressive "higher race." The process of elevating natives, of making them over in new pattern, is never a happy one for the native. The wrenching of old ties, the destruction of old ideals, the replacing of an ancient life by one different in every detail, is a painful thing.

I deplore atrocities, but I have often thought that, if I were a member of a race that was being improved by outside influences, I would rather they should kill me outright with bullet or with knife than subject me to the suffering of years in molding me to new ideas. In other words, I sometimes feel that flagrant outrage is less painful to the victim than well-meant direction, teaching, and elevation to their object.

Let us turn, however, to the whole subject of atrocities.

XI.

January 30, 1907.

MUCH has been said of flogging and the chicotte. There is no question that flogging is general throughout the Congo Free State. The English word "flogging" is one which is generally known and understood by officials of every nationality throughout the country; it is known, too, by a surprising number of natives. The chicotte is known to everybody within the state limits—its name is Portuguese. In all my journey in the Congo, while I frequently heard the word "flogging" and constantly heard the word "chicotte," I never heard the French term for either. Nor do I think the native has. It is plain that neither flogging nor the chicotte was introduced by Belgians. These found them in the country on their arrival, introduced by English and Portuguese.

It is not the fact of flogging in itself that raises objections; not only the state and traders but the missionaries find it necessary to whip their black employés. In fact, at a missionary conference—I think it was—one missionary referred laughingly to the boys whom another (by the way, one of the chief witnesses against the state) "had flogged into the kingdom of heaven." He did not mean the boys had died as a result of the flogging, but simply that they had found salvation through its means. It is, then, the amount, severity, and undeservedness of the whipping which are reprobated.

I saw, of course, plenty of flogging. Not, indeed, with such an instrument as has been recently shown throughout the United States by a complaining missionary. I was conversing recently with a friend who had been profoundly stirred in connection with Congo atrocities. He happened to mention the chicotte, then said: "Have you ever seen a chicotte? You know it is made of six thongs of hippopotamus skin, twisted tightly together." I told him that I had seen hundreds of chicottes, but that I had never seen one such as he described. As a matter of fact, I have seen chicottes of a single thong, and of two or three twisted together, but I have never seen one composed of six. I do not know whether such an instrument would cause greater suffering in punishment, but it certainly is better suited for display to sympathetic audiences who want to be harrowed by dreadful reports. The first flogging that I happened to see was at a distance. I was busy measuring soldiers; hearing cries, I looked in the direction whence they came, and saw a black man being publicly whipped before the office of the commissaire. An officer of proper authority was present inspecting the punishment, which I presume was entirely legal.

In the second flogging which I witnessed, this time at close quarters, I was myself implicated to a degree. We were at a mission station. The mission force and practically all the people from the place were attending Sunday morning service. It was fruiting time for the mango trees, which were loaded with golden fruit. Suddenly we heard an outcry, and in a moment the mission sentry, delighted and excited, came up to our veranda with an unfortunate prisoner, whom he had taken in the act of stealing fruit. He insisted on leaving him with us for guarding. I turned him over to my companion, who set him on his veranda, telling him to stay there until the missionary should come from the service.

The prisoner squatted down upon the veranda without a word of discussion, laying the fruit, evidence of his guilt, upon the floor at his side. We were so angry at him that he made no attempt at escaping, and did not even eat the fruit which he had stolen, that we washed our hands of the whole affair, and believed he deserved all that might be coming. The service over, the missionary appeared, accompanied by the triumphant sentry. When the prisoner had admitted his guilt, the missionary asked whether he preferred to be sent to the state for punishment or to be whipped by him, to which the prisoner replied that he should prefer the mission flogging.

With great formality the instrument of punishment was produced; it consisted of two long and narrow boards, perhaps six feet in length and two or three inches wide; between them was fixed a board of the same width, but of half the length. At one end these were firmly screwed together, while the other end was left open. It will be seen that when a heavy blow was given with the instrument the free ends of the two long sticks would strike together, producing a resounding whack which, no doubt, produced a psychic suffering in the victim in addition to the true physical pain. However that may be, fifteen blows, I think, were administered, and the prisoner discharged.

One day, upon the Kasai steamer, we witnessed a wholesale whipping, which was typical of this mode of punishment as regularly administered. The night before we had been forced to tie up beside the forest. The night was dark and the cutters refused to make wood for the next day's journey. This was a serious act of insurrection, involving delay and trouble. When, finally, the next morning the wood had been loaded and the steamer was under way, ten of the rebels were marched up to the captain. In turn each lay down upon the floor, a friend held his hands and wrists, while the capita administered twenty blows. It is comparatively rare that the white man himself does the flogging; usually it is the regular capita who is in charge of the workmen, or a special one of the working force detailed to play the part.

It makes a notable difference in the way in which the punishment is received whether the hands are firmly held to prevent struggling. An English-speaking white man not in the government or company employ, who had had more or less opportunity for observation in our Southern states, and whose experience in the Congo extends over several years, told me that flogging with the chicotte was a rather mild and simple punishment; that it hurt but little, and that, for his part, he preferred to hit the workmen on the head and kick them in the shins, those being places more tender to the application than the part subjected to the chicotte. On the whole, I am inclined to think that there was something in what he said. It is certain that in most cases the suffering from a flogging is momentary. I have even seen persons undergoing serious flogging exchange significant glances and signals with their friends, in which the suggestion of pain was quite absent. Many a time, also, I have seen a man immediately after being flogged, laughing and playing with his companions as if naught had happened. Personally, though I have seen many cases of this form of punishment, I have never seen blood drawn, nor the fainting of the victim.

It is common to speak of the chain-gang with great sympathy. One sees chain-gangs at every state post; it is the common punishment for minor offenses to put the prisoner on the chain. Sometimes as many as twelve or fifteen are thus joined together by chains attached to iron rings placed about their necks. They are employed in all sorts of work—bringing water for use about the station, sweeping roads, clearing fields, carrying burdens. On our arrival at a state post, immediately after we had presented our introductions to the commandant, the chain-gang would be sent to bring our freight and baggage to the rooms to which we were assigned. The ring around the necks of these prisoners is a light iron ring, weighing certainly not to exceed two pounds. The weight of chain falling upon each prisoner can hardly be more than six or eight pounds additional. In other words, the weight which they are forced to carry in the shape of ring and chain does not exceed, probably does not equal, ten pounds.

From the viewpoint of service rendered, the chain-gang has little value. It dawdles, lags, idles, and plays; only when it is carrying burdens does it really work. I have never seen a chain-gang composed of women, nor have I seen women on the same gang with men. It is stated by the missionaries that such things occur. Certainly, every one would object to the chaining together of male and female prisoners. Apart from this, the chain-gang does not particularly arouse my sympathy. It is a very mild form of punishment, and one which, of course, is common in as bad a form or worse throughout many of our Southern states. To grieve over the weight carried in the form of chain and ring is simply ridiculous; there are to-day thousands of women among these Congo tribes who for the sake of decoration carry about their neck a heavy ring of brass weighing twenty, twenty-five, or thirty pounds. It is no uncommon thing for both men and women to have a weight of thirty, forty, or fifty pounds of brass and iron rings and ornaments upon them.

I cannot believe that the ordinary flogging, such as I have seen, causes notable suffering to people who, for purposes of decoration or treatment of rheumatism, submit without evidence of pain to such operations as I have described in detail in an earlier article. Nor can I feel that the mere fact of carrying chain and ring of less than ten pounds' weight involves terrible suffering for people who regularly carry much heavier burdens of ornaments.

Much has been said of late in regard to hostages. The taking of hostages and holding them until some obligation or agreement had been performed was a common native custom. Stanley frequently captured women and children, or even men, of tribes in the districts through which he was passing and held them as hostages until they should show him the trail he should follow, or until their people supplied him with the food or other things which he desired. At the ill-fated Yambuya camp the rear guard frequently seized the women of the natives who had failed to bring in food supplies in return for the trade stuffs offered. This seizure of hostages is mentioned repeatedly in the writings of the early travelers, and seems to have caused no outcry on the part of the sensitive civilized world at that time. Why should it now?

It is a common practice, though a disagreeable one to us, for one who sells a thing to keep back a part of it in making delivery of the goods. On one occasion we bought a musical instrument, a marimba, which consisted, in part, of a dozen gourds as resounding bodies. Every one of these gourds was necessary to the instrument, yet the seller, after we had examined it with care to see that it was perfect, removed three of the gourds, in accordance with this custom. The instrument was sent to us by the son of the seller's chief, old Chicoma. When we found the instrument at home we at once noted the absence of the three gourds. Old Chicoma's son had a companion with him. We at once decided to hold the chief's son as a hostage, sending word by his companion that he would be set free only on the appearance of the missing gourds. When we told the youth that we had "tied him up," that being the expression for holding a person hostage, he looked sheepish, but made no complaint, recognizing the justice of our action.

This was at 4 o'clock in the afternoon. He made no attempt to escape, although we had not in any way actually interfered with his freedom of movement. We gave him supper when the time came and breakfast in the morning. He found his stay tedious, however, and finally, when none was looking, slipped away. He must have met the messenger bringing the missing gourds before he was any distance from the house, as he appeared with our property about half an hour after the flight.

The only other personal experience in the matter of hostages that we had was in the High Kasai. A white man, agent of the Kasai company, was our guest for the night. In the early morning our friend, Chief Ndombe, appeared, in great excitement, begging us to loan him cloth, as the white man had seized one of his slaves and would not release him until he had fully paid a debt which the white man claimed he owed him. The question appeared complicated, and we let him have the cloth, after which we went over to hear the palaver accompanying the payment. Both sides told their story, with much gesticulation. The white man's boy had owned a woman, for whom he claimed to have paid six pieces of cloth; she had run away, and he had sought in vain for her. The chief, old Chicoma, told him that the woman was at Ndombe and in the house of the great chief. So they seized Ndombe's slave—a little lad about 11 years of age, whose bright face and curious head shaving always had greatly attracted me. This boy our visitors were holding as a hostage until Ndombe should produce the woman or pay her value.

Of course, the whole procedure was illegal, and I was inclined to take up the matter vigorously. There were, however, so many elements of doubt in the matter that I finally concluded to let it pass. Of hostages held by company agents or by state people we saw but few, and never learned the circumstances under which they had been taken. They were rarely in actual confinement, and we saw no evidences of bad treatment toward them. In native custom, the hostages are regularly well treated and fed regularly, while held in captivity. While we have never seen maltreatment of hostages, we can readily understand how such could arise. Taken, as they usually are, in order to force the bringing in of food or forest products, if their holding does not produce the desired effect the feeling of vexation resulting may easily lead to cruelty.

MEN SENTENCED TO THE DEATH PENALTY FOR MURDER
AND CANNIBALISM, BASOKO

XII.

January 31, 1907.

PEOPLE in this country seem to expect that every traveler in the Congo must meet with crowds of people who have had one or both hands cut off. We have all seen pictures of these unfortunates, and have heard most harrowing tales in regard to them. Casement, the English consul, whose report to the British government has caused so much agitation, and who described many cases of mutilation, himself saw[A] but a single case; and that case, though put forward by the missionaries as an example of state atrocities, was finally withdrawn by them, as the subject had not been mutilated by human assailants, but by a wild boar. Casement traveled many miles and spent much time in securing the material for his indictment, and yet saw[B] but this one case. We saw a single case of mutilation. It was a boy at Ikoko, probably some twelve years old. He had been found, a child of three or four years, by the side of his dead mother, after a punitive expedition had visited the town. His mother's body had been mutilated and the child's hand cut off. We might have seen a second case of this sort at this place if we had searched for her. There is a second there.

No one, I think, would desire to excuse the barbarity of cutting off the hands of either dead or living, but we must remember that the soldiers in these expeditions are natives, and in the excitement and bloodthirst roused by a military attack they relapse to ancient customs. There has, indeed, been considerable question recently whether the cutting off of hands is really a native custom. Sir Francis de Winton, himself an Englishman, and Stanley's successor in the administration of the Congo State, says that it was. And Glave says: "In every village in this section (Lukolela) will be found slaves of both sexes with one ear cut off. This is a popular form of punishment in an African village. It is not at all unusual to hear such threats as 'I will cut your ear off,' 'I will sell you,' or 'I will kill you,' and often they are said in earnest." Where such customs were constant in native life it is not strange that they have lasted on into the present.

Of course, in this connection we must not forget that mutilation of dead bodies is not by any means confined to the Congo Free State, nor to its natives. Only a few months ago, in Southern Africa, the British force cut off the head of a hostile chief. When the matter was investigated, the excuse given was that it was done for purposes of identification, and that the body was afterwards brought in and buried with it.

The most of the difficulty with the natives of the Congo Free State, of course, comes in connection with the demand to gather rubber. The native hates the forest; he dislikes to gather rubber; it takes him from his home, and comfort, and wife. We have never accompanied a party of natives gathering rubber, but we have seen them started and have also seen them bringing in their product. The best rubber of the Congo is produced by vines which frequently grow to several inches in diameter. The same vine may be tapped many times. The milky juice, which exudes abundantly, promptly coagulates into rubber; as it hardens it is rolled into balls between the palm and some portion of the body, such as the chest or leg.

The place where we have seen most of rubber production is in the High Kasai, where the famous red rubber is produced, which sells for the highest price of any African caoutchouc. My missionary friends have told me that conditions in the Kasai are not bad and that they have no special fault to find with the Kasai company. While there were things that might be criticised, there was apparent fairness in the business. The natives waited several days after they had gathered their balls of rubber before bringing them in. This was for the reason that the company's agent had but an unattractive stock of goods in his magazine at the moment; they preferred to wait until a new stock should come up on the expected steamer. As soon as it appeared they sent word that they might be expected the following day.

The old Bachoko chief, Maiila, was brought in state, in his blue hammock; his people came singing and dancing with the baskets full of balls of rubber on their heads. All proceeded to the magazine, where the great steelyards were suspended and the rubber weighed; each man looked carefully to see that his stock balanced evenly, and one of their number, who understood the instrument and could figure, stood by to see that all went fair. While the rubber was a demanded tax, a regular price of 1 franc and 25 centimes the kilo was paid. This was given in stuffs, of course, and the native selected what he pleased from the now abundant stock of cloths, blankets, graniteware, and so forth. It may truly be said that they came in singing gayly and went home glad.

At Mobandja we saw a large party setting out to the forest to gather rubber, different from any that we had seen before in that a considerable number of women formed a part of it. This feature I did not like, although I presume it is an effort to meet the criticisms of the report of the royal commission of investigation. The commission particularly criticised the fact that the men, in going into the forest, were deprived of the company of their women—a hardship strongly emphasized. It is surely a mistake, however well it may be meant, to send the women into the forest with the men to gather rubber. Such a procedure involves the neglect of her fields and interrupts the woman's work.

And here we touch upon the thing which in my opinion is the worst feature of the whole Congo business. Anything that affects the woman's work necessarily brings hardship. I have seen many heart-rending statements in regard to the loss of work time which the man suffers by going to the forest to gather rubber. We are told that by the time he has gone several days' journey into the dense forest, gathered his balls of rubber, and returned again to his village, he has no time left for work, and his family and the whole community suffers as a consequence. But from what work does this gathering of rubber take the man?

We have already called attention to the fact that the support of the family and the actual work in any village fall upon the woman. The man, before he went into the forest to gather rubber, had no pressing duties. His wife supported him; he spent his time in visiting, dancing, lolling under shelters, drinking with his friends, or in palavers, sometimes of great importance but frequently of no consequence; in other words, he was an idler, or a man of leisure. I feel no sorrow on account of the labors from which he is restrained. Personally, I should have no objection to his idling. If he does not want to work and need not work, I see no reason why he should not idle. But my readers are practical men, who talk much of the dignity of labor and the elevation of the lazy negro. Very good; if work is dignified and the elevation of the negro necessary, let him collect rubber, but do not mourn over the fact that he is deprived of opportunity to earn a living for himself and family.

There is, indeed, one set of circumstances under which the man may really be deprived of opportunity to aid in the work of gaining a living. Where the men in a community are really fishermen—they are not always so—to take them from their fishing entails a hardship.

The thing which seems to me the worst is the kwanga tax on women and the fish tax on men. The former is at its worst, perhaps, in Leopoldville; the latter is bad enough at Nouvelle Anvers. Leopoldville is situated in a district which yields much less for food than necessary. It has always been so. Even in the days before the white man came, the people in the native villages on Stanley Pool were obliged to buy food supplies from outside, as they themselves, being devoted to trading, did no cultivation. With the coming of the white man, and the establishing of a great post at Leopoldville, with thousands of native workmen and soldiers to be fed, the food question became serious. The state has solved the problem by levying a food tax on the native villages for many miles around.

The women are required to bring a certain amount of kwanga—native cassava bread—to Leopoldville within a stated period of time. To do this involves almost continuous labor, and really leaves the women little time for attending to the needs of their own people. Some of them are forced to come many miles with the supply of bread. When they have cared for the growing plants in their fields, prepared the required stint of kwanga, brought it the weary distance over the trails, and again come back to their village, they must begin to prepare for the next installment. For this heavy burden there must certainly be found some remedy. Personally, it seems to me that the women belonging to the workmen and the soldiers might be utilized in cultivating extensive fields to supply the need. The condition of the men who pay the fish tax is analogous to that of these kwanga-taxed women.

The question of the population of the Congo is an unsettled one. Stanley estimated it at 29,000,000 people; Reclus, in 1888, estimated it at something over 20,000,000; Wagner and Supan claimed 17,000,000, and Vierkandt sets the figure at 11,000,000. The governor-general, Baron Wahis, who has several times made the inspection of the whole river, is inclined to think that even Stanley's figure is below the true one. Between these limits of 11,000,000 and 29,000,000 any one may choose which he prefers. No one knows, or is likely for many years to know. Those who believe that Stanley's figure was true in its time, and that Vierkandt's is true at present, may well insist, as they do, that depopulation is taking place.

Personally, I have no doubt that depopulation is going on. Of course, the enemies of the Free State government attribute the diminution in population chiefly to the cruelties practiced by the state, but it is certain that many causes combine in the result.

The distribution of the Congo population is exceedingly irregular. From Stanley Pool to Chumbiri there has been almost no population during the period of our knowledge. On the other hand, from Basoko to Stanley Falls the population is abundant and there is almost a continuous line of native villages along the banks for miles. Practically, the state of population is really known only along the river banks. Back from the riverines are inland tribes, the areas of which in some cases are but sparsely settled, while in others they swarm. They are, however, little known, and just how the population is distributed is uncertain. The district which we personally best know—the Kasai—is one of the most populous of all the Congo State, and around the Sankuru, one of the main tributaries of the Kasai, we perhaps have the densest population of the country. If we take Stanley's estimate as accurate, the population would average twelve to the square kilometer.

Among known causes for the diminution of Congo population we may mention first the raiding expeditions of the Arabs. These were numerous and destructive in the extreme, throughout the region of the Upper Congo and the Lualaba. Organized for taking slaves and getting booty, they destroyed ruthlessly the adult male population and deported the women and children. Towns were burned and whole districts left unoccupied. There is no question that many of the punitive expeditions of the state have been far more severe than necessity demanded; "the people must be shown the power of Bula

Matadi." It is said that Vankerckhoven's expedition destroyed whole towns needlessly in the district of Chumbiri and Bolobo. Certainly, the population in this section was formerly abundant. Everywhere along the shores one sees the groups of palm trees marking the sites of former villages; probably the present population is no more than one fourth that which existed formerly.

Throughout the whole district, where the French Congo touches on the river, it is a common thing for timid or disgruntled villagers to move *en masse* across the river into French territory. These wholesale removals are an advantage to the natives, as that portion of the French Congo is less well occupied by white posts and government officials than the corresponding part of the Congo Free State. The natives who have thus removed unquestionably have an easier time in the French colony. This, however, can hardly be called depopulation, as it involves no loss in persons, but merely a transfer from the Free State side to the other. It does not at all affect the actual number of the race.

Sleeping-sickness is carrying off its tens of thousands.

But after we suggest these causes we are still far from a full solution of the problem of depopulation, which is a mysterious thing. In Polynesia we have another example of it on a prodigious scale. In Polynesia we have neither slave raids, nor punitive expeditions, nor sleeping-sickness. Yet, adults die and children are not born. If things continue in the future as in the past, the time is not far distant when the Polynesian—one of the most interesting and attractive of human races—will be a thing completely of the past.

The case of our own American Indians is similar. Whole tribes have disappeared; others are dying out so rapidly that a few years will see their complete extinction. I am familiar with the arguments which, from time to time, are printed to demonstrate that the number of American Indians is as great as ever. It seems, however, that it is only rich tribes that hold their own; the reason is not far to seek, but we may not here pursue the argument further.

[A] I am here in error. Casement *saw* more than one case of mutilation; he carefully *investigated* but one.

[B] See footnote A.

XIII.

February 1, 1907.

NOR is apparent depopulation of the Congo a matter of recent date. Quotations might be given from many travelers. We quote three from Bentley, because he was well acquainted with the country and because he was an English missionary. In speaking of the town of Mputu, an hour and a half distant from San Salvador, he describes the chief, Mbumba, a man of energy, feared in all his district. He was strict in his demands regarding conduct. In his presence others were required to sit tailor-fashion. "To ease the cramped limbs, by stretching them out before one, is a gross breach of decorum; any one who did so in Mbumba's presence was taken out, and was fortunate if he lost only an ear. We have known several great chiefs who would order a man who sat carelessly to be thus mutilated. His own people were much afraid of him on account of his cruel, murderous ways; for a small offense he would kill them relentlessly. He was superstitious and very ready to kill witches. Through his evil temper, pride, and superstition, his town of several hundred people was reduced to eighty or ninety souls."

Again he says: "Our next camp was at Manzi; but as we had so many people, the natives preferred that we should camp in a wood at Matamba, twenty minutes' walk beyond the town. The wood marked the site of a town deserted some years before. There were no other towns on the road from there to Isangila, a distance of thirty miles, for the wicked people had killed each other out over their witch palavers. This was what the natives told us themselves. Yet they went on killing their witches, believing that if they did not do so all the people would be exterminated. Two wretched villages of a few huts each were to be found a few miles off the path, but the country was practically depopulated."

In another place he says, in speaking of the caravan days: "All the carriers suffered acutely from fever, and this was the case with all the caravans on the road. This mortality was largely increased by the improvidence of the carriers themselves. Thousands of men were engaged in transport work at the time, but very few troubled to carry enough food with them, or money wherewith to buy it. As a rule, the young men staid in their towns as long as they had anything to buy food with; when they failed, they borrowed until their debts became too great. Then they arranged to go with some caravan to carry, and received ration money for the road. This would be partly used up in the town, and the rest go to those from whom they borrowed. On the road they lived largely on palm nuts and raw cassava, and returned to their homes in a terribly exhausted condition. With the influx of cloth gained by transportation came hunger, for wealth made the women lazy; they preferred to buy food rather than produce—the gardens came to an end, then hunger followed, and sickness and death. Women staid at home to mourn, and the mischief became worse. Sleep-sickness and smallpox spread. The population of the cataracts district is not more than half what it was fifteen years ago. The railway is now complete, and the country will adapt itself to its new conditions."

Those who are hostile to the state, of course, will find great comfort in this quotation; for the transport system was an introduction by the Belgians. It will be observed, however, that the author mentions no cruelty on the part of the new masters in this connection; it must also be remembered that the missionaries were as much interested in the caravan system as any, and assisted in its development. My chief object in introducing the quotation is to show how impossible it is to affect native conditions in one way without bringing about a connected series of changes, not always easy to foresee.

To me, the real wonder is that there are any of the Congo peoples left. Think of the constant drain due to the foreign slave trade, continued from an early date until after the middle of the last century. Think of the continuous losses due to the barbarism of native chiefs and demands of native customs—to wars, cannibalism, execution, and ordeal. Think of the destruction caused by punitive expeditions—towns burned, people killed. Think of the drafts made by the caravan system and the public works which the state has been forced to carry out. Think of the multitudes who have died with the diseases of the country and from pestilence introduced by the newcomers. Yet the population really shows signs of great vitality to-day, and the most discouraged missionary hesitates a real prediction for the future.

There is a most interesting and suggestive map in Morel's new book, "Red Rubber." It bears the legend, "Map showing revenue division of the Congo Free State." Upon this map we find marked with little crosses the localities where specific reports of atrocities have been received. The distribution of these crosses is interesting. We find a concentration of them along the main river from the Rubi River almost to the mouth of the Kasai, a notable bunch of them in the region of the A. B. I. R., and in an area worked by the Antwerp trust; also in the district of Lake Leopold II. There are few crosses indicative of bad treatment in the Congo above this district, and practically none in the lower Congo and the Kasai. It is precisely in the areas where these crosses are so frequent that the early travelers had difficulty with the natives in first traversing the country. In other words, the districts where native hostility has in recent years produced the acts of alleged cruelty have always been centers of disturbance and attack against the white man. Districts which were found occupied by peaceful and friendly tribes have been the scenes of few outrages. This seems to me a point worthy of serious consideration.

For my own part, I believe that any well-behaved white man can to-day traverse Africa in every direction without danger as long as his journey confines itself to areas of Bantu and true negroes. Livingstone practically had no trouble with native tribes; Schweinfurth, entering from the Nile, penetrated to the heart of Africa with little trouble; Du Chaillu traveled throughout the Ogowe valley without difficulty with natives; Junker, following Schweinfurth's trail, penetrated farther into what is now the Congo Free State, passing through the territory of many warlike and cannibal tribes, but never armed his men and never had a difficulty with any native chief. It is true, however, that the tribes of the Congo differ vastly from each other in disposition. Some are warlike, some are peaceful to cowardice; some are genial, friendly, open; others are surly, hostile, reserved, treacherous. While I have always felt that Stanley looked for trouble and that he left a trail of blood unnecessarily behind him, I recognize that the Bangala and many of their neighbors are less agreeable, less kindly, more disposed for trouble than many of the other tribes in the Free State. It is precisely with these tribes that the chief difficulties of the state have been.

Another curious point is shown on Morel's map. From what has been said by critics of the state we would be justified in expecting to find those districts where the white man's influence had penetrated most fully, and where he himself existed in greatest number, the worst in the matter of atrocity. But it is precisely in these districts that Morel's map shows no marks of reported atrocities. It is plain, then, that the officials of the Congo Free State are not, as a body, men delighting in cruelty and outrage. Where there are numbers of them, instead of conditions being at their worst they are at their happiest. It is only where there are lonely men surrounded by depressing influences and in the midst of hostile and surly tribes that these dreadful things are found. It is natural to expect that with fuller penetration of the white men into these districts conditions will change hopefully.

But why should we pick out the Congo Free State for our assault? Atrocities occur wherever the white man, with his thirst for gold, comes into contact with "a lower people." He is ever there to exploit; he believes that they were created for exploitation. If we want to find cruelty, atrocities, all kinds of frightful maltreatment, we may find them in almost every part of negro Africa. They exist in the French Congo, in German Africa, in Nigeria, even in Uganda. If we insist on finding them, we may find cruelty, dispossession, destruction of life and property, in all these areas. The only ruthless act involving the death of a black native that we really saw was in French territory. If there were any object in doing so, we could write a harrowing story of British iniquity in Africa, but it is unnecessary; every one who stops to think and who reads at all knows the fact.

Wherever British trade finds native custom standing in its way, we shall find cruelty. Why was King Ja Ja deported? I have heard an interesting incident connected with his case. One who for many years has voyaged up and down the western coast of Africa tells me that while Ja Ja was still at his height of power the natives of his district, paddling near the shores in their canoes, were always happy and joyous. Ja Ja stood in the way of the British traders gaining so much money as they wanted, and so he was exiled and taken a prisoner to distant lands. From the day of his departure the happiness of life was gone from all the country. Few natives put out in their canoes, and those who did were silent; the song and laughter of former days were hushed. Until the day when he was brought home, a corpse, for burial, somberness and sadness settled down upon his people, before so gay and light hearted. What was it caused the trouble at Benin but British greed insisting on opening up a territory which its natives desired to keep closed? The Benin massacre that followed was dreadful, but it did not begin to compare in frightful bloodshed with the punitive expedition which followed—a feat scarce worthy of British arms. What was the cause of hut-tax wars? What is the matter now in Natal? Do we know all that goes on in Nigeria? Wherein is excellence in the expropriation of lands and products in Uganda for the benefit of concession companies of the same kind exactly as those in Congo? Why is it worse to cut off the hands of dead men for purposes of tally than to cut off the heads of dead chiefs for purposes of identification? But let it pass—we are not undertaking an assault on Britain.

XIV.

February 2, 1907.

RETURNED from the Congo country and a year and more of contact with the dark natives, I find a curious and most disagreeable sensation has possession of me. I had often read and heard that other peoples regularly find the faces of white men terrifying and cruel. The Chinese, the Japanese, other peoples of Asia, all tell the same story.

The white man's face is fierce and terrible. His great and prominent nose suggests the tearing beak of some bird of prey. His fierce face causes babes to cry, children to run in terror, grown folk to tremble. I had always been inclined to think that this feeling was individual and trifling; that it was solely due to strangeness and lack of contact. To-day I know better. Contrasted with the other faces of the world, the face of the fair white is terrible, fierce, and cruel. No doubt our intensity of purpose, our firmness and dislike of interference, our manner in walk and action, and in speech, all add to the effect. However that may be, both in Europe and our own land, after my visit to the blacks, I see the cruelty and fierceness of the white man's face as I never would have believed was possible. For the first time, I can appreciate fully the feeling of the natives. The white man's dreadful face is a prediction; where the fair white goes he devastates, destroys, depopulates. Witness America, Australia, and Van Diemen's Land.

Morel's "Red Rubber" contains an introductory chapter by Sir Harry Johnston. In it the ex-ruler of British Central Africa says the following: "A few words as to the logic of my own position as a critic of King Leopold's rule on the Congo. I have been reminded, in some of the publications issued by the Congo government; that I have instituted a hut-tax in regions intrusted to my administration; that I have created crown lands which have become the property of the government; that as an agent of the government I have sold and leased portions of African soil to European traders; that I have favored, or at any rate have not condemned, the assumption by an African state of control over natural sources of wealth; that I have advocated measures which have installed Europeans as the master—for the time being—over the uncivilized negro or the semicivilized Somali, Arab, or Berber."

It is true that Sir Harry Johnston has done all these things. They are things which, done by Belgium, are heinous in English eyes. He proceeds to justify them by their motive and their end. He aims to show a notable difference between these things as Belgian and as English. He seems to feel that the fact of a portion of the product of these acts being used to benefit the native is an ample excuse. But so long as (a) the judge of the value of the return made to the sufferer is the usurper, and not the recipient, there is no difference between a well-meaning overlord and a bloody-minded tyrant; and (b) as long as the taxed is not consulted and his permission is not gained for taxation, there is only injustice in its infliction, no matter for what end. Sir Harry uses the word "logic." A logical argument leaves him and Leopold in precisely the same position with reference to the native.

Sir Harry closes his introduction with a strange and interesting statement. He says:

"The danger in this state of affairs lies in the ferment of hatred which is being created against the white race in general, by the agents of the king of Belgium, in the minds of the Congo negroes. The negro has a remarkably keen sense of justice. He recognizes in British Central Africa, in East Africa, in Nigeria, in South Africa, in Togoland, Dahomey, the Gold Coast, Sierra Leone, and Senegambia that, on the whole, though the white men ruling in those regions have made some mistakes and committed some crimes, have been guilty of some injustice, yet that the state of affairs they have brought into existence as regards the black man is one infinitely superior to that which preceded the arrival of the white man as a temporary ruler. Therefore, though there may be a rising here or a partial tumult there, the mass of the people increase and multiply with content and acquiesce in our tutelary position.

"Were it otherwise, any attempt at combination on their part would soon overwhelm us and extinguish our rule. Why, in the majority of cases, the soldiers with whom we keep them in subjection are of their own race. But unless some stop can be put to the misgovernment of the Congo region, I venture to warn those who are interested in African politics that a movement is already begun and is spreading fast which will unite the negroes against the white race, a movement which will prematurely stamp out the beginnings of the new civilization we are trying to implant, and against which movement, except so far as the actual coast line is concerned, the resources of men and money which Europe can put into the field will be powerless."

This is curious and interesting. But it is scarcely logical or candid. Allow me to quote beside Sir Harry's observations the following, taken from the papers of March 4, 1906:

"Sir Arthur Lawley, who has just been appointed governor of Madras, after devoting many years to the administration of the Transvaal, gave frank utterance the other day, before his departure from South Africa for India, to his conviction that ere long a great rising of the blacks against the whites will take place, extending all over the British colonies from the Cape to the Zambesi. Sir Arthur, who is recognized as an authority on all problems connected with the subject of native races, besides being a singularly level-headed man, spoke with profound earnestness when he explained in the course of the farewell address: 'See to this question. For it is the greatest problem you have to face.' And the solemn character of his valedictory warning was rendered additionally impressive in the knowledge that it was based upon information beyond all question."

It is certain that the affairs in the Congo Free State have produced neither restlessness nor concerted action in British Africa. Why is it that on both sides of Southern Africa there have been recent outbreaks of turbulence? The natives, indeed, seem ungrateful for the benefits of English rule. Sir Arthur Lawley looks for a rising over the whole of British Africa, from the Cape to the Zambesi. In what way can the misgovernment of the Congo by its ruler have produced a condition so threatening? Both these gentlemen have reason, perhaps, for their fears of an outbreak, but as I have said, there is neither logic nor candor in attributing the present agitation in Southern Africa to King Leopold.

What really is the motive underlying the assault upon the Congo? What has maintained an agitation and a propaganda with apparently such disinterested aims? Personally, although I began my consideration of the question with a different belief, I consider it entirely political and selfish. Sir Harry Johnston naïvely says: "When I first visited the western regions of the Congo it was in the days of imperialism, when most young Britishers abroad could conceive of no better fate for an undeveloped country than to come under the British flag. The outcome of Stanley's work seemed to me clear; it should be eventually the Britannicising of much of the Congo basin, perhaps in friendly agreement and partition of interests with France and Portugal."

Unquestionably this notion of the proper solution of the question took possession of many minds in Great Britain at the same time. And England was never satisfied with the foundation of the Congo Free State as an independent nation.

A little further on, Sir Harry states that the British missionaries of that time were against such solution; they did not wish the taking over of the district by Great Britain. And why? "They anticipated troubles and bloodshed arising from any attempt on the part of Great Britain to subdue the vast and unknown regions of the Congo, even then clearly threatened by Arabs." In other words, Britons at home would have been glad to have absorbed the Congo; Britons on the ground feared the trouble and bloodshed necessary. But now that the Belgians have borne the trouble and the bloodshed and paid the bills, Britain does not despise the plum. Indeed, Britain's ambitions in Africa are magnificent. Why should she not absorb the entire continent? She has Egypt—temporarily—and shows no sign of relinquishing it; she has the Transvaal and the Orange Free State; how she picked a quarrel and how she seized them we all know. Now she could conveniently annex the Congo.

The missionaries in the Congo Free State are no doubt honest in saying, what they say on every possible occasion, that they do not wish England to take over the country; that they would prefer to have it stay in Belgian hands; that, however, they would have the Belgian government itself responsible instead of a single person. I believe them honest when they say this, but I think them self-deceived; I feel convinced that if the question was placed directly to them, "Shall England or Belgium govern the Congo?" and they knew that their answer would be decisive, their vote would be exceedingly one-sided and produce a change of masters. But the missionaries are not the British government; they do not shape the policies of the empire; their agitation may be useful to the scheming politician and may bring about results which they themselves had not intended. It is always the scheme of rulers and of parties to take advantage of the generous outbursts of sympathy and feeling of the masses for their selfish ends.

The missionaries and many of the prominent agitators in the propaganda against the Free State have said they would be satisfied if Belgium takes over the government. This statement never has seemed to me honest or candid. The agitators will not be suited if Belgium takes the Congo; I have said this all the time, and the incidents of the last few days have demonstrated the justness of my opinion. Already hostility to Belgian ownership is evident. It will increase. When the king really turns the Congo Free State government into Belgium's hands the agitation will continue, complaints still will be made, and conditions will be much as formerly.

Great Britain never has been the friend of the Congo Free State; its birth thwarted her plans; its continuance threatens her commerce and interferes with expansion and with the carrying out of grand enterprises. In the earlier edition of his little book entitled "The Colonization of Africa," Sir Harry Johnston spoke in high terms of the Congo Free State and the work which it was doing. In the later editions of the same book he retracts his words of praise; he quotes the atrocities and maladministration of the country. My quotation is not verbal, as for the moment I have not the book at hand, but he ends by saying something of this sort: "Belgium should rule the Congo Free State; it may safely be allowed to govern the greater portion of that territory."

"The greater portion of the territory"—and what portion is it that Belgium perhaps cannot well govern? Of course, that district through which the Cape-to-Cairo Railroad would find its most convenient roadbed. If Great Britain can get that, we shall hear no more of Congo atrocities. There are two ways possible in which this district may be gained. If England can enlist our sympathy, our aid, our influence, she may bid defiance to Germany and France and seize from Leopold or from little Belgium so much of the Congo

Free State as she considers necessary for her purpose, leaving the rest to the king or to his country.

If we are not to be inveigled into such assistance, she may, in time and by good diplomacy, come to an understanding with France and Germany for the partition of the Free State. Of course, in such event France would take that section which adjoins her territory, Germany would take the whole Kasai, which was first explored and visited by German travelers, and England would take the eastern portion, touching on Uganda and furnishing the best site for her desired railroad.

The same steamer which took me to the Congo carried a newly appointed British vice-consul to that country. On one occasion he detailed to a missionary friend his instructions as laid down in his commission. I was seated close by those in conversation, and no attempt was made on my part to overhear or on their part toward secrecy. His statement indicated that the prime object of his appointment was to make a careful examination of the Aruwimi River, to see whether its valley could be utilized for a railroad. The second of the four objects of his appointment was to secure as large a volume as possible of complaints from British subjects (blacks) resident in the Congo Free State. The third was to accumulate all possible information regarding atrocities upon the natives. These three, out of four, objects of his appointment seem to be most interesting and suggestive.

On a later occasion I was in company with this same gentleman. A missionary present had expressed anxiety that the report of the commission of inquiry and investigation should appear. It will be remembered that a considerable time elapsed between the return of the commission to Europe and the publishing of its report. After the missionary had expressed his anxiety for its appearance and to know its contents, the vice-consul remarked: "It makes no difference when the report appears; it makes no difference if it never appears; the British government has decided upon its course of action, and it will not be influenced by whatever the commission's report may contain." Comment upon this observation is superfluous.

Upon the Atlantic steamer which brought us from Antwerp to New York City there was a young Canadian returning from three years abroad. He knew that we had been in the Congo Free State, and on several occasions conversed with me about my journey. We had never referred to atrocities, nor conditions, nor politics. One day, with no particular reason in the preceding conversation for the statement, he said: "Of course, the Belgians will lose the Congo. We have got to have it. We must build the Cape-to-Cairo road. You know, we wanted the Transvaal. We found a way to get it; we have it. So we will find some way to get the Congo."

Of course, this was the remark of a very young man. But the remarks of young men, wild and foolish though they often sound, usually voice the feelings and thoughts which older men cherish, but dare not speak.

CONSTRUCTING NEW HOUSES AT BASOKO

XV.

February 3, 1907.

OUGHT we to interfere? In this whole discussion I have looked at the question solely from the humanitarian standpoint. I assume that Secretary Root's first presentation of the matter was carefully prepared. He insisted that we had no grounds for interference, insofar as the Berlin conference was concerned. It is only, then, from the point of view of interest in the natives, the desire to save them from suffering and from atrocity, that we can join with England in calling a new conference of the world's powers to consider Congo matters. Ought we to pursue such a course? We ought not, and that for several reasons.

First—We should not interfere in Congo matters from philanthropic reasons, unless we are ready to undertake the policing of the whole of Africa. If the atrocities in the Congo are sufficient to involve us in difficulty with Belgium or with Belgium's king, the atrocities and cruelty practiced in the French Congo, throughout German Africa, in the Portuguese possessions, and even in the English colonies, must also attract our notice. If we really intervene to save the African black man from white oppression, we must do this job thoroughly and on a large scale.

Second—We should not interfere with the conditions in Congo unless we desire strained relations with France and Germany. No possible agitation will bring about a second meeting of all the powers that participated in the Berlin conference. Turkey alone, so far, has signified her willingness to act with England. The only other nation in which there seems to be the slightest trend toward participation is Italy. No Scandinavian country—Sweden, Norway, Denmark—will join in the movement. The many Scandinavians who, in one capacity or another, have labored in the Congo Free State are, on the whole, well satisfied with the conditions. Though there is a vigorous and aggressive Swedish mission in the country, it is significant that its members have never joined in the agitation. Nor is Holland, which has sent a large number of individuals into the Congo State as employés of government and concession companies, likely to favor an agitation. Austria, for various reasons, stands aloof. France has a definite understanding whereby in case of the dissolution of the Congo Free State she becomes heir to all the district. Germany, responsible for the foundation of the Congo Free State, has, on the whole, always favored its existence, and would certainly oppose interference in its affairs. In case of the partition of the Congo, Germany would be willing enough to take her share, but it is really more to her interest both at home and abroad to maintain its independence. All these European countries speak quite freely in regard to England's design. France and Germany would seriously oppose any demonstration by England and the United States.

Third—We ought not to interfere unless we are really willing to play the undignified part of pulling England's chestnuts from the fire. What would we, nationally, gain by the partition of the Congo? Our repeated declarations about not wishing new territory in distant regions are, of course, looked upon as twaddle by other nations. If we really mean them, we must avoid the very appearance of evil. What will the natives gain by partition? They will still have their oppressors, only they will be divided around among three instead of being exploited by one. Suppose the redistribution did take place. Suppose France, Germany, and England divided the Congo between them; suppose—as would be certain—that oppression and atrocity continued in the divided territory. Would we still continue our noble effort in behalf of the suffering black millions?

Fourth—We should not interfere, unless we wish to present a glaring example of national inconsistency. Distance lends enchantment to the view. We are solicitous about the Bantu in their home under the rule of Leopold II.; we have 12,000,000 or more of them within our own United States. The Bantu in the Congo we love. We suffer when he is whipped, shudder when he is put upon a chain-gang, shriek when he is murdered. Yet, here he may be whipped, put on the chain-gang, murdered, and if any raise an outcry he is a sentimentalist. Our negro problem is a serious and difficult one. We do not know how to treat it. But it is at our door, and we can study it and strike out some mode of treatment. But the years pass, and we do nothing. So complicated is it and so united together and interdependent its issues and its elements, that any course of action is dangerous, because we frequently cannot foresee the outcome of well-meant effort. With this example constantly before us, one would suppose that we would hesitate in meddling with the equally complicated problem, regarding conditions of which we know little or nothing, on the other side of the globe.

Fifth—We ought not to interfere, unless we come with clean hands. We have an even closer parallel to Congo conditions than our negro problem in the South. In the Philippines we found a people to be elevated; an inscrutable Providence—so we say—thrust the Philippine Islands, with their millions, upon us. A few years ago we heard much of benevolent assimilation. Benevolent assimilation is the most dreadful of all forms of cannibalism. Our Congo reformers emphasize the fact that the Congo State was founded with many philanthropic assertions and with high-sounding promises of improving and elevating the native population. The parallel is close. We took the Philippines and Filipinos for their good. So we said. Of course, we took them just as the European nations have taken Africa—for exploitation. Had there been no hope of mines, of timber, of cheap land for speculation, of railroads to be built, and other enterprises to be undertaken and financed, we should never have had such a tender interest in the advancement of the Filipinos. And how has our benevolent assimilation proceeded? Just exactly as it always proceeds everywhere in tropic lands with "lower peoples." Torture, punitive expeditions, betrayal of confidence and friendship, depopulation—these have been the agencies through which we have attempted to elevate a race.

You will tell me that what I am about to quote is ancient history and has lost its force. It is no more ancient than the bulk of the atrocities and cruelties within the Congo. We quote a newspaper of April 12, 1902:

"From the Philippines authentic news is now at hand tending to confirm the charges of barbarity on the part of American army officers, which have hitherto been strenuously and sweepingly denied. This news comes in Associated Press dispatches reporting the court-martial trial of Major Waller, now in progress at Manila. This officer led an expedition last winter into the interior of the island of Samar. After being given up for dead, he and his party returned to camp January 28th, delirious from privation. Major Waller was next heard of in this connection in a dispatch of March 6th from Manila. He had been subjected to court-martial proceedings, on charges of having, while on this ill-fated expedition, executed natives of the island of Samar without trial. One of the specifications alleged that in one instance the accused had caused a native to be tied to a tree, and on one day to be shot in the thigh, on the next in the arm, on the third in the body, and on the fourth to be killed. Friends of Major Waller attributed his horrible action to delirium caused by privation; but Major Waller himself refused to make this defense, insisting that he had acted under superior authority."

This sounds like an indictment of the Belgians in the Congo put forth by the Congo Reform Association. It is revolting; it is horrible; it probably is true. Personally, I believe that Major Waller must have suffered from the physical, the mental, the moral disintegration which the tropics so constantly produce in white men. It is unlikely that he was by nature a man of exceptional cruelty. He became what he was—either permanently or for a time—through the environment in which he lived. He had excuse; so have the Belgians. There is another respect in which this quotation sounds Congo-like. Major Waller insisted that he had "acted under superior authority."

This phrase, he "acted under superior authority," is constantly harped upon by Morel and others of the Congo agitators. Much is made of it, and we are constantly asked to trace home the order which issued from superior authority From whom came Major Waller's orders? In his trial, February 8th, 1902, he disclosed the startling nature of General Smith's orders, as he had understood them. He swore that General Smith had said: "I wish you to kill and burn. The more you kill, the more you will please me. The interior of Samar must be made a howling wilderness. Kill every native over ten years old."

When serious complaints of maladministration are brought before the Belgian authorities of the Congo, investigation and trial are usually ordered. The Congo agitators lay great stress upon the fact that in the Congo these trials are farces; that the accused is rarely sentenced to punishment; that sometimes after his acquittal he is lionized, made a hero of, advanced in office. This is an unpardonable crime when committed by the Belgians. Lothaire—and really Lothaire was as bad as any—was thus treated. One would imagine from the chorus of complaint along this line that every English or American officer accused of cruelty, misgovernment or maladministration was promptly and severely punished.

Major Waller received the verdict that he had acted "in accordance with the rules of war, the orders of his superior, and the military exigencies of the situation." This, again, can hardly be improved upon in all the cases put forward joyously by the reformers. When complaint is made it is never treated honestly. There is always whitewashing. Why howl over Belgian failure to punish? Waller's verdict shows that we do precisely the same thing in the same circumstances. But look at what was done with General Smith, the man who ordered that down to ten years of age the natives should be killed. He, too, was ordered to undergo court-martial. From a newspaper of May 3d, 1902, we quote: "At the opening, Colonel Woodruff announced his willingness to simplify the proceedings by admitting that most of the accusations were true. He said he was willing, in behalf of General Smith, to admit that inasmuch as the country was hostile, General Smith did not want any prisoners, and that he had issued orders to Major Waller to kill all persons capable of bearing arms, fixing the age limit at ten years, because many boys of that age had borne arms against the American troops, and that he had ordered Major Waller also to burn the homes of the people and to make Samar a howling wilderness."

What was done with General Smith? His court-martial began on April 25. Its result was, of course, a whitewash; it always is, whether the person tried is American, French, German, or Belgian. It is curious, however, to observe how others were affected by this case. There was one man who knew better than any other all the facts relating to the Philippines. His utterance, which we shall quote, was expressed, indeed, before this trial, but it was expressed with full knowledge of similar facts. That man, on March 5th, made the assertion: "It is not the fact that the warfare in the Philippines has been conducted with marked severity; on the contrary, the warfare has been conducted with marked humanity and magnanimity on the part of the United States army." What a pity that we are less ready to talk of marked humanity and magnanimity of others! Can Waller's crime be surpassed by anything from Congo; can any order be more cruel than General Smith's?

I have said that this would be called ancient history. At Leopoldville I asked about atrocities; the response was that at present there was nothing serious to complain of in that region beyond the kwanga tax; when I reached Ikoko, where undoubtedly many cruel things have taken place, they told me that at present such things did not occur there, that to find them I must go to the A. B. I. R.; that the fish tax was too heavy, but that of cruelties, atrocities and mutilations there had been none for years. At Bolobo I heard precisely the same story—the most frightful things had taken place at Lake Leopold II.— that recently nothing serious had happened at Bolobo itself. I presume that there are outrages and cruelties of recent date in the A. B. I. R. and the Antwerp Concession. But here, again, the parallel between the Congo and the Philippines is close. While the Waller and Smith incident is ancient, there is plenty doing at the present time. We quote a paper August 18, 1906: "The Pulajanes—wild tribesmen of the Philippine island of Leyte—continue their fighting. Five Americans, including a lieutenant and a surgeon, were killed in a hand-to-hand encounter in the town of Burauen on the 9th. It was reported on the 14th that Governor-General Ide has determined to exterminate the Pulajanes, even if it should take every American soldier on the islands to do it."

This sounds like depopulation. And why is depopulation worse in Africa than in the Philippines? Why should a President who views the latter with complacency—and I may say with commendation—feel so keenly with reference to the former? A special message of commendation was promptly sent to an American leader for his killing of hundreds of men, women, and children; depopulation on a large scale and of the same kind as he reprobates when done by Leopold's soldiers. Our friends of the Congo Reform Association are strangely silent in regard to such letters of commendation; they are much grieved because Lothaire was lionized, but they hurrah over the accumulating honors of a Funston.

When our hands are clean and when we have given the Filipinos their well-deserved independence and free government, and left them to work out their own salvation, then and not till then, should we intervene in the Congo Free State for reasons of humanity. I say when we have left the Filipinos to work out their own salvation; we have strange ideas regarding the kindnesses we do to other peoples. Thus Cuba is supposed to be under an eternal debt of obligation to us for the government which we set up in that unhappy land. We devised a model government, according to our own ideas; to be sure, it is a government so expensive to keep up that few, if any, portions of the United States with the population of Cuba could possibly support it. We put in sanitary improvements, nominally for the benefit of Cubans, but actually with a shrewd afterthought for ourselves, which we demanded should be maintained at any price. Of course, it is impossible for a country with the population and resources of Cuba to maintain them. This will give us repeated opportunities for interference in the affairs of the island, interference which ultimately may weary the people into assent to uniting with us. They will lose both independence and happiness, and we will gain an added problem; and the only persons profited will be those who are, and will be, exploiting the island for their selfish ends.

So, in the Philippines, we will develop a government which, theoretically, may seem perfect. The difficulty is that it must be much less suitable for Filipinos than a less perfect government, planned and carried out along lines of their own ideas. Lately a Filipino in this country has said something which has the ring of truth. "We have money enough to maintain a better and less expensive government than that costly one which is trying to make the people what the government wants them to be, and not to make itself what the people want and expect, dictating laws one day which next day are canceled and changed in a thousand places and in a thousand ways, so that justice is converted into a mere babel. Believe me, dear sir, that even our ephemeral government at Malolos showed no such incapacity. This is due to the fact that he who governs the house does not belong to the house, and everybody knows the old Spanish proverb, 'The fool is wiser in his own house than the wise man in his neighbor's.'"

If it is necessary for us as a nation to look for African adventure; if to give a strenuous President the feeling that he is "doing something" we must meddle in the affairs of the Dark Continent, there is a district where we might intervene with more of reason, and consistency, and grace than we are doing by going to the Congo. We once established on African soil, whether wisely or not I do not intend to discuss, a free republic for the blacks. In Liberia we have an American enterprise, pure and simple. It has not been a great success. It is just possible—though I doubt it—that Liberia would at several times have profited and been advantaged by our instruction and interest. But it seems to possess little interest for us. Just now, like the Congo, it is attracting British attention. Whether it has large or little value, whether it possesses great opportunities or not, it is now a center of interest to Great Britain. She does not need our help in pulling chestnuts from the fire there, and there has been strange silence and ignorance in this country regarding it as a new sphere for English influence. If we assist England in expanding her African possessions at the expense of the Congo Free State, Liberia will be the next fraction of Africa to succumb to English rule. England's methods of procedure are various. It might be a useful lesson for our statesmen and politicians to study Liberia's prospects with care. We are still young in the business of grabbing other people's lands. England could teach us many lessons. The latest one may well be worthy our attention, since, in a certain sense, it deals with a district where we naturally possess an interest.

Milton Keynes UK
Ingram Content Group UK Ltd.
UKHW042108131124
451149UK00006B/698